SO-CALLED CHRISTIAN

HEALING SPIRITUAL WOUNDS LEFT BY THE CHURCH

SO-CALLED CHRISTIAN

HEALING SPIRITUAL WOUNDS LEFT
BY THE CHURCH

JIM TURNER

AMBASSADOR INTERNATIONAL
GREENVILLE, SOUTH CAROLINA & BELFAST, NORTHERN IRELAND

www.ambassador-international.com

So-Called Christian
Healing Spiritual Wounds Left by the Church

© 2014 by Jim Turner
All rights reserved
Author Photo by Vienna Jacobson,
www.TriumphAssistance.com

ISBN: 978-1-62020-264-7
eISBN: 978-1-62020-365-1

Cover design and page layout: Hannah Nichols
E-book conversion: Anna Riebe

AMBASSADOR INTERNATIONAL
Emerald House
427 Wade Hampton Blvd.
Greenville, SC 29609, USA
www.ambassador-international.com

AMBASSADOR BOOKS
The Mount
2 Woodstock Link
Belfast, BT6 8DD, Northern Ireland, UK
www.ambassadormedia.co.uk

The colophon is a trademark of Ambassador

ENDORSEMENTS

"IF THE CHURCH'S INABILITY TO manage its diversity is the illness, then Jim Turner has diagnosed it with beauty and transparency and prescribes the treatment for it as well! If you are a leader (lay or clergy) in the church, you must read this book."

Blake Coffee, Executive Director of Christian Unity Ministries, Author of *The Five Principles of Unity* and *Trusting God's People . . . Again.*

"'DON'T GO TO THAT CHURCH. Their view of baptism is kooky.'

'PASTOR, YOUR SERMON LAST SUNDAY bordered on heresy! How can you condone that abominable music the Christian radio stations play?'

'IF THAT'S WHAT YOU THINK about when the rapture occurs, I can't fellowship with you anymore.'

'YOU DRINK ALCOHOL AND STILL consider yourself a Christian?'

AND SO IT IS THAT the self-appointed leukocytes of the body of Christ launch their search-and-destroy missions against any other cells that don't sport the same theological genotype they do. Pride, the lust for power, misdirected focus and misplaced zeal have caused God's people to turn on each other rather than unite and battle the true disease: Satan and his pathological infections. Why has the Church's immune system turned AIDS-like in its fanatical quest to kill the "disease" within? Is it any wonder that this dysfunctional body is shriveling, and an increasing number of people elect to stay quarantined from it?

IN THE TRADITION OF DR. Gregory House of television fame, Pastor Jim Turner draws from his years of experience in ministry and in God's Word to identify the true causes of the disease and to formulate a brilliant plan to save the patient. Turner's plan is not new, but evidently forgotten by most. God knew from ages past that conflicts were going to arise among His people. In His foresight, He prescribed practical ways to resolve them and carefully laid His directions out in His Word . . . where they have been largely ignored for years. Turner—and God's Spirit—breathe life into these principles and present them here for anyone who would rather reflect Christ's ideal of love and unity, rather than the prevalent discord that seems to characterize Christianity nowadays."

Chris Adsit – President: Disciplemakers International
National Director: Branches of Valor
Author: *Personal Disciplemaking; Connecting With God*

"IN HIS FIRST BOOK, JIM Turner speaks direct into the core of critical dysfunction within the body of Christ. Digging deep into very personal life experiences, Jim has aggressively spoken into a troubling issue that permeates Christianity today. Engaging and easy to read, *So-Called Christian* is a revealing personal account that every believer should read. Thank you Jim for going where few would go!"

Troy Meeder, Owner and Co-Founder of Crystal Peaks
Youth Ranch and author of *Average Joe: God's
Extraordinary Calling to Ordinary Men*

"THIS COMPELLING VOLUME WILL CHALLENGE the way you think about your doctrine, Church bodies other than your own, and your commitment to the Gospel of Jesus Christ—a challenge 21st Century Christianity sorely needs if it is to speak once again with relevance, authenticity, and power."

Matthew L Jacobson, President, Loyal Arts, Elder, Tumalo
Bible Fellowship, www.MatthewLJacobson.com

CONTENTS

ACKNOWLEDGEMENTS

I would like to gratefully acknowledge my sweet wife, a true healer who suffers deep wounds. May Jesus Himself touch her more deeply than any wound can penetrate. Without her character, holy example, and ideas, I would have little to say.

I would like to thank Sam and Tim Lowry at Ambassador for their partnership in publishing this work. They have been persistently encouraging at every turn and a true joy to work with. Thanks also to J.P. Brooks, editor par excellence! His work brought mine to life in many places. His experience and gentle hand have added much to this book!

Additional thanks are due to my friend Matt Jacobson, whose patience, instruction, and encouragement helped refine and focus the book's theme and direction. Thanks also to all those who endured several readings of the manuscript: Blake Coffee, Bob Bolander, Robert Vincent, Randy Worland, Vicki Bayless, Bill Gannon, Chris Adsit, Chris Wick, Kent Estell, Burnell Johnson, Timothy Bailie, Troy Meeder, and others who faithfully read and coached me on several points. Blessings to all I've mentioned and to the many others who have influenced me both in reference to this work and in my walk with Christ. I'm deeply indebted to all of you.

Thanks above all to my Lord and Savior Jesus Christ, who continues to do a relentless work on a tough and brittle piece of stone. I'm looking forward to seeing my Sculptor when the work is done!

PREFACE

I WRITE THIS AS THE Chief of Sinners in the area of arrogant self-confidence and angry, manipulative expression. Being "right" has been my idol for most of my life. I have sinned and offended many of God's most precious saints. I am the man of whom Jesus says a millstone should be hung about his neck and he be drowned in the depths. I have been the "so-called" Christian. Anything you read here that may be of help is because God in His mercy decided to save me twice: once when I confessed Christ, and again when I confessed a black pride that had come to define me.

The second salvation came with a crushing revelation of what I had become. Pride is an utter darkness that blinds our soul. It is an internal calamity that keeps us distracted with others' faults so we cannot see our own. I was planted firmly in this deep-black blindness. When light broke into my darkness, I was ashamed and disgusted with myself. The realization electrocuted my view of myself. I was not the man I wanted to be, but something foul and small. I knew myself to be the opposite of truly Christian. I knew that every command toward relationship in the Scriptures lay broken at the door of my heart. It is dreadful when God shows us how sinful we really are.

I'm telling this ugly side of the story first so that you will know that pride, whether it be doctrinal, preferential, or self-protective, brings great pain. I can't even describe the depths of pain others have suffered due to my pride. Relationships are precious, so to lose even one is a tragedy. Furthermore, the process of putting back together a shattered relationship is so much harder than the process of humbling ourselves before God.

I write this as a human being, crying out to people like me. I beg you to kill your pride before you kill others with it. What is written here will help you, but only if you die to yourself, as Jesus commands us to do. The Bible tells us to mortify, or kill, "the members of our earthly body." I will tell you that if you belong to God and refuse to kill your own sin, He will do it for you, and the pain is excruciating at the deepest levels of the soul. I would advise you not to push Him. He loves you too much to allow you to destroy yourself with pride. He loves His Bride too much to allow you to destroy her.

In spite of my sinful failings, I believe that God has graciously given me hope that I can yet be of some use to Him. He still loves me. He loves His Bride. He is jealous for her. He provides careful instruction for her proper treatment and for her members to love one another. You'll find hope here for your situation. Close relationships often bring pain closer. They also bring true love closer—close enough to taste and feel and revel in. May God's love find you.

INTRODUCTION

ASK ANYONE. ANYONE, THAT IS, who has been involved in church or Christian ministry for any length of time. "Have you ever been hurt by a fellow believer?" Or ask, "Have you ever felt judged, belittled, or resigned to a second class Christian status by another believer?" Or, "Do you feel distant from another believer over his insistence that you agree with his standard, his conscience on a matter, or her particular brand of Christianity?" Or, "Have you ever found yourself in an uncomfortable conversation or heated argument while trying to convince someone toward a specific point of view on a spiritual topic?"

Further, have you ever been accused of breaking a spiritual standard, or "going liberal," or being Puritanical, or not standing for the Faith, or not being Spirit-filled, or using a substandard Bible version, or any other such peculiarity? These accusations cut deep and often leave us questioning our acceptance before God. Perhaps you've been discarded by an individual or group of believers because you didn't meet up to a set of spoken or unspoken directives that may or may not have solid Biblical foundations. If so, you have been on the receiving end of one of the

13

most destructive influences in the Church. You have experienced a sort of attack. You may feel maimed, defaced, ashamed, unqualified, unloved . . . fill in your own adjective. In short, you've been labeled a "so-called" Christian because you didn't meet up to an artificial standard.

Did you know that nearly four out of ten (37%) of non-churchgoing Americans state the reason they do not attend church is due to negative past experiences with churches or church people?[1] And the estimate of non-churchgoing people in America is 100,000,000. That's 37,000,000 people claiming to be hurt by professing Christians! That's a lot of hurt! World War II claims conservatively to have cost 40,000,000 lives worldwide. The spiritual casualties in America alone are enough to rival that war. The disturbing and alarming thing about it is that ours is a civil war—we are battling ourselves. The statistic mentioned only includes those who no longer attend. What about those who have been hurt but hang in there? How big is that number? Are you numbered among the wounded? Or maybe worse, have you been the aggressor?

Lest we get wrapped up in the hurt we've experienced and stay there, let's remember that the Lord has given us clear instructions on what to do in these instances. We cannot remain a hurting, out-of-fellowship, "Lone Ranger" Christian. God has called us to be an active part of something much bigger, to rise above our hurt, and to strive for things lofty and joyful. We are called to recognize our past, recover from it or repent of it, and learn how to overcome the next threat to our joy in Christ. There's the important distinction—recover from it or repent of it. Depending on what side we were on, we will have to do one of the two.

---

1   "Millions of Unchurched Adults Are Christians Hurt by Churches But Can Be Healed of the Pain," Barna Group, 2010, accessed Jan. 12, 2014, https://www.barna.org/barna-update/article/12-faithspirituality/362-millions-of-unchurched-adults-are-christians-hurt-by-churches-but-can-be-healed-of-the-pain#.UqeI66WBopE.

I've experienced both being a wounder (yes, I know it's not a real word, but you get the picture) and wounded. Judgmental and judged. A labeler of brothers in Christ and, likewise, labeled a "so-called" Christian. What's worse, I don't now hold as essential some of the things I used to contend so vehemently for. Memory does not serve to remind me of all the "Biblical" issues that I felt were so important that they needed to be defended. Regretfully, how I handled them is all too memorable.

In the past, usually after a heated argument over a minor topic, my typical response regardless of which side of the fence I was on at the time was to pray for the other party (usually with mental condescension) and then avoid the issue in the future. It was the "spiritual" way to handle these things, I thought. I was normally very satisfied with my own stand on whatever the issue was, being always pretty sure of my understanding about what the Bible said on the topic. In a very self-protective way I tended to put the blame on the other party, their misunderstanding, their immaturity in the faith, their pride, their disobedience, their whatever.

Not anymore. I mean—and this is an important caveat—not when I'm walking in obedience to Christ and the Scriptures.

That's the point. When I'm walking in obedience to Christ and the Scriptures, I handle things much differently.

The reason for this change is that I discovered one of the most intriguing truths in the Bible.

Much of what I was experiencing and causing others to experience violated one of the most basic of all Christian virtues, one that Christ Himself was most passionate about. How I missed it for some twenty years of my walk with God I don't know, but miss it I did. In those years I completely failed to notice one of the most common and poignant repeated themes in the New

Testament concerning the Church, the Bride of Christ, the Body of Christ, which all believers are a part of.

It's really embarrassing to have not seen it earlier. It's seemingly everywhere, plainly written and plainly illustrated in the lives of the apostles and the early church. It's the bright white background on which the entire beauty of the Church stands out in full color. It's the often undetected but necessary quality that emphasizes the Gospel to the unbelieving world. It is a genetic trait shared with the Holy Trinity, effected in us by the Spirit, and worked out in obedient, Spirit-led, Bible-immersed believers.

What did I miss? The most basic truth: that real, Spirit-begotten Love produces Unity among brothers and sisters, and that Christian Unity is the burning passion of Christ.

God is patiently at work in this revelation, and we will benefit by paying attention. These truths will save grief in our relationships with other believers, while giving us insight into God's heart for us personally. They will also open up for us a great window on the character of God Himself. And knowing God's character not only comforts us, it also empowers us to live out our Christian walk in the light of who God is and how He acts; it enables us to become more and more like Jesus.

CHAPTER ONE

DISEASE AND DESPERATION

MY FAMILY HAS A DEAR loved one who has suffered greatly from an unseen disease. The disease, though invisible, has been the source of pain in body, mind, and soul. Those of you who have encountered chronic disease may realize the effects that disease has on every aspect of life; and conversely, how every aspect of life may affect the disease. Outside pressures, stress, emotional turmoil, diet, climate, relationships, and a host of other influences can contribute to the cause, duration, and intensity of a disease. Those who suffer from chronic illness, along with those who love them, find themselves having to learn to deal with a tremendous number of painful realities. Some of them so deeply hurtful, that we wish to run away and be spared the pain of dealing with them forever.

The lessons themselves may not linger as important or informative to us, but the method by which they are taught is crucial. The Lord has many instructors—only a few of them human. The circumstances we learn under are often as instructive as the conclusions we reach. It was this way in the case of my loved one.

The disease manifested itself in separate storms. It was not illness like a cold or a flu, but ill as in debilitating, not-able-to-live-a-normal-life ill. The fact that it was unseen made treatment elusive.

As the years went by, this person endured uncounted doctor visits, treatments, uncontrollable weight loss, days in bed with no energy, complete cash drain, feelings of inadequacy, questions from friends and relatives, and all the associated issues that go along with a persistent disease. There would be seasons of improvement, but then long stretches of difficulty and discouragement. Loving friends and family found themselves engulfed at times in thoughts that spun them into places they never imagined having to go. It is deeply discouraging to look on suffering and not be able to find a way to help.

Life went on. New homes, good jobs, a good church, and other signs of normal life were continually being added—but never any permanent relief for the illness.

There were moments of great hopelessness when the family would think, "This is the way it's going to be for the rest of our lives. We need to get used to it." Sometimes we would think, "What if this ends in death?" But most of the time, being optimists, we kept thinking things would get better for our beloved.

They didn't.

You may be intimately acquainted with the physical, mental, emotional, and spiritual battles that have to be fought to endure and cope with the daily grind of persistent disease. For those of you who are not, let me throw back the curtain. Whatever despair looks like to you, imagine it living in your mind: always a shadow on everything you do; always pecking away at your hopeful thoughts; always grinding at your heart; always bringing out your most glaring flaws—anger at trivialities, overbearing demands on innocent bystanders, rash decisions, numbness to true love, inability to feel and sense God or to pray, blindly going about the days' chores and not remembering their content. Both those who suffer disease and those close to them endure these various experiential peaks and valleys.

After years of struggling and maintaining a tenuous hold on health, the disease became catastrophic. From a healthy 105 pounds, weight dropped to 80; our dear one's countenance was pallid and weak. Clothes hung on them like sheets on a clothesline. Days were spent in bed. It was then that the diagnosis of full-blown Crohn's disease came.

I have come to realize that my blind pride and overbearing legalism made every part of this person's suffering worse, and most likely even played a part in causing the troubles from the start. I won't elaborate on that except to point you back to my foreword. I caused a lot of people pain.

I COULDN'T SEE MYSELF AS THE MONSTER THAT I HAD BECOME.

If I had it to do over again with what I know now, I think I could have been a healer, but instead I made everything worse. I was utterly sightless; I didn't examine myself at all. I blamed something else, or dismissed self-incriminating ideas altogether. I was a monster who couldn't see himself in the mirror and so remained ignorant of the damage I was doing. I just kept stumbling along in the dark while others were suffering from my sin. I wish

I could tell you that a miracle happened and God changed me, but that didn't happen for twenty-five years.

The point came when there were no options. Friends and family were begging for something to be done. Some were shocked that nothing more was being done, but no one really knew what to do. All were exasperated, exhausted, and desperate.

This was an incredibly elusive disease. There was plenty of advice from professionals, but none of them had the answer. As of this writing, no drugs, treatments, or surgeries have been found to actually cure the disease. The medications and treatments weren't even keeping the symptoms at bay. A normal diet wasn't possible: no wheat, no dairy, no corn, no sugar was allowed. Sometimes it didn't matter what or how much was eaten, it seemed to pass through in miserable pain, scraping against the raw internal wounds of the digestive system, causing intense cramping, and leaving no health benefit.

You might imagine all the ramifications of this. The emotional pressure of wanting relief from the crisis and finding none was a constant weight and added worry. To this person's credit, they always mustered the strength to show true affection. They maintained the sweetest of spirits and clung incredibly tightly to the Lord. Some of the most precious of God's promises came in the darkest hours of those years. The Lord was not slack in His promises in those days or now, but the reality of His workings is sometimes more mist than stone. In this life, experiencing what we know to be true is often elusive. We must walk by faith.

Those traumatic days caused many of us close to this person to learn a lot about the nature of this disease, and we have since learned even more. But knowing the nature of the disease still brought no relief. Something unusual was needed: a miracle, a treatment that might have been unorthodox, but one that would work—at least for this precious one.

To end the suspense—a treatment was finally found. Unorthodox, unusual, but immediate help was found to lift this blessed child of God out of the most desperate hour and onto a path of restorative healing that is being enjoyed even today. This person made it through the "crucible of grace" by God's enduring mercies. He healed, He restored, He rescued, He reclaimed. No disease, whether physical or spiritual, has Him baffled or powerless!

If you are familiar with the diagnosis, you know that both ulcerative colitis and Crohn's disease fall into a specific category of ailments. As a result of knowing this person and their disease, I have since recognized that the nature of these types of disease is an illustrative gift from God.

To the point. The difficulty of the circumstances is not the point. The desperateness of the experience isn't the point. The suffering endured and the lessons learned from the suffering are not the point. Not that disease doesn't teach us enough to fill a barge. But that's all in addition to what is really instructive about the experience.

THE CHURCH IS SUFFERING FROM AN AUTOIMMUNE DISEASE.

The greatest lesson comes from the disease itself. The disease is a marvel! That may sound sick (pardon the pun), but I have learned as much from studying the nature of the disease as I have from witnessing the suffering it brings.

Ulcerative colitis, Crohn's, and a host of other ailments are called *autoimmune* diseases. What causes them is a mystery in almost every case. Their effect on the body is fairly well known, though, and researchers have been obliged to start with the effects and work backward to the cause. One day perhaps, someone will find the cause and then effect the cure.

What we know presently is that no external antigens have been found that are consistently the primary causes of these diseases. This is contrary to most diseases. In autoimmune diseases, no virus, bacteria, or other foreign body has been found to be the culprit. We are not studying what a foreign body does to us. The great wonder and the most fascinating study is what these diseases cause our bodies to do to themselves!

The pathology of these autoimmune diseases is incredibly instructive for the Church, the Body of Christ. So let's consider that Body for a moment.

What would you say is the most debilitating, Christ-dishonoring, witness-destroying menace (disease) to the Church today? Can you put a finger on why the Church, the Body of Christ at large, has lost its effectiveness in the world? Why are people leaving churches in droves and ignoring (even militating against) the voice of the Christian Church in society, as if we are the bad guys? Who is to blame for this exodus and this outspoken resistance?

Is it the liberal higher educational establishment with its elevation of science as the arbiter of truth? The disdainful claim that says, "If it can't be proven by the scientific method then it is to be discarded as myth!"? Is it the general breakdown of ethics, from the halls of government all the way down to the local paperboy? Is it the undying desire to get ahead using any means possible: a philosophy that cannot stomach a Church that will hold society to a standard of honesty?

Is it the speeding slide toward atheistic socialism in our governments? Or is it the prevalence of aggressive atheism itself? Or maybe it's the subtler undercurrent of apathy in a society distracted by entertainment and bloated by ease? Taking another tack, could it be the breakdown of the family, skyrocketing divorce, fatherless and motherless children, and the general disregard for moral living arrangements?

Let's not leave the media and Hollywood out. Don't you suspect that the ceaseless warfare on decency and the relentless push against every moral boundary has had its effect on the Church? Are the all-out efforts to sow doubt and spin truth as myth and mystery causing the foundations of the Church to crumble?

Or could there be something more insidious and pervasive, something more penetrating and difficult to eradicate? Are we facing a menace larger than amoral government, secularized education, the mindless pursuit of success, family breakdown, and media manipulation?

But how could that be? Surely the items I've listed are the most effective armies arranged in battle against the Church today? Aren't they?

Not according to Jesus.

According to Jesus, the menace is . . . me.

Collectively, it's us. The Church. His Own Bride. The beam is in our eye, the blood on our hands. We are attacking ourselves. The Church is suffering from an autoimmune disease. We are participating in a self-inflicted spiritual mutilation that has had many consequences: some apparent, some hidden.

I suspect that these are difficult words to swallow, since I haven't yet told you the nature of the trespass. And these external problems have done great harm to the Church, so to turn the blame inward might seem wrong to you. Plus, I've said there is no real cause or source on which to pin this disease. But if there's no blame to attach to an outside source, then this leaves us grasping for something.

No cause? No cure? What am I getting at?

What I am getting at is what individuals in the Body can do to address this "no cause, no cure" ailment that is systemically destroying the Church, and therefore is destroying the work of Christ in the world. I say "no cure" very carefully and with the understanding that Jesus can cure any ailment. There is a cure, but the disease is so intrusive and insidious that we had better look at managing the symptoms in the short term, and pray for Jesus to effect permanent healing in the long term.

When I say insidious—I mean deadly. When I say intrusive—I mean it invades or affects every part of the Body. Whatever the origin, whatever the consequences, the truth is that the Body is its own enemy, completely contrary to its created purpose.

This is the one thing we were shocked to hear about our loved one's disease. They were told, "Your body is attacking itself. It's damaging, destroying, and mutilating its own tissue." When asked why, the doctors didn't know. They couldn't pin it down or give an exact cause. If they had, I'm sure they would have eradicated the cause immediately.

This is where the Church stands. We love to track down causes—compromise, or false doctrine, or evil influence from outside—so we can eradicate them and have a pure church. But what if the cause can't be located? What do we do then? Do we allow the Body to go on attacking itself, just because we can't determine the root of the problem?

In many cases of physical disease, what the patient believes and the way they think about themselves and their circumstances, while not the cause of disease, certainly exacerbates the symptoms and allows the disease to become more debilitating. In much the same way, the Church entertains false notions about herself and thus exacerbates, even perpetuates, her own illness.

This book is an appeal to individual believers and to the Body of Christ to recognize that we have a disease—an autoimmune disease. This disease makes our Lord and us unattractive, pallid, weak, and ineffective.

Believers are complicit in the destruction of the Gospel witness, and we need to repent of our sin and be restored to a vibrant, living testimony in line with what the Lord Jesus Christ originally planned for us. We need to stop attacking ourselves. It's time to stop the excuse making and start dealing stubbornly with the sin. How can we deal with sin lightly, anyway? If my family's loved one had dealt with the disease lightly, I'm fairly certain they would not be healthy today. The disease was serious and demanded some serious steps be taken to deal with it, steps this person has to maintain even today in order to keep it in check. Sin is like that. It's the most serious ailment with which we humans have to wrestle. As Christians, sin should be approached with the most ardent and straightforward language possible. The Church must face her sin in this way. We must constantly and vigilantly guard against this ever-encroaching disease.

The sin I'm speaking of is the weakening and possible destruction of Gospel witness in the world. That's serious! I'm charging that Christians—not the devil, not the world, but Christians—are responsible for the deterioration of the Gospel witness among men on earth.

Looking for the cause of the Church's disease is similar to looking for the cause of any of the autoimmune diseases we have referred to in our illustration. Apart from the general label of Man's Sinfulness, we are not going to get deeply into causes in this book. Also similar to autoimmune diseases, we probably will not find any guaranteed cure, at least not on this side of eternity. What we will do is explore a way to overcome the effects of the disease, and to live in the harmony and love that Jesus intended for His Bride. We will discover the Biblical prescription for living out healthy spiritual lives within the context of diversity and difference. We will find the solution to the Church's anemic Gospel witness in the world. We will empower Christians at all levels with a workable solution for living abundantly in the midst of a fallen world and a divided church.

The beautiful thing is that God knew that we would struggle with disagreements. He knew exactly what issues we would wrestle with, which ones would divide us, which ones would tempt us to despise one another, and which ones would split the Church age after age. None of them are a surprise to Him. He anticipated every possible nuance of partition in the Body and addressed them even before they arose. He informed the Apostle Paul just how to handle controversy between brothers.

It is the responsibility (and should be the passion) of every true believer to see the witness of Jesus restored in power to a world that so desperately needs Him.

Differences between brothers should not hinder us in the pursuit of our duty. If we will obey, the day will come when the Church realizes the irresistible influence of the Gospel on men's hearts. Envision the Church displaying power like that displayed in the second chapter of Acts. The key to a return to that kind of power lies very plainly in the Scriptures—in the words of Jesus Himself. Like a secret key to inexhaustible treasure, it's just waiting to be discovered. Once we find it and use it, this key will unlock the limitless power of Christ to work through His church, and so persuade the souls of men to meet Him at the foot of the cross and proceed to the glory of His throne.

THE BIBLE'S PRESCRIPTION FOR A HEALTHY SPIRITUAL LIFE INCLUDES LARGE DOSES OF CHRISTIAN DIVERSITY.

CHAPTER TWO

JUST IGNORE IT;
IT WILL GO AWAY

AN AUTOIMMUNE DISEASE IS A disease that occurs when the body's immune system sees its own body or a part of its body as an enemy. It then attacks itself, mutilating and destroying otherwise healthy tissue.

So what's all this got to do with the Church? Much, in every way, I assure you.

The Church (all believers everywhere) is defined in Scripture as the Body of Christ. We'll use the illustration of the body to reflect how disease can do damage and create an unattractive figure. If the Church (the Body) is unattractive, diseased, and divided, we can expect that the outside world will react to it in predictable ways: ways that are clearly anticipated in the Scriptures. We can also expect our Lord to have something to say about it.

The Bible is, in essence, "the doctors' orders" or "the treatment plan" for our autoimmune disease. Not only is the disease addressed in Scripture, but the treatment plan is also well documented. Instructions for maintaining health in the Body abound. In fact, God explains to us how we can thrive in the midst of this challenging Church health issue. He gives us hope and practical steps for healing the Body. These instructions apply Body-wide. They are applicable on a personal, local church, denominational, and para-church ministry level.

In other words, what the Bible has to say about the topic at hand applies to every believer, denomination, movement, creed, color, confession, ministry, etc., regardless of its distinctives or divisions. In fact, it is the distinctives or divisions that define these denominations, movements, creeds, colors, and confessions that we are addressing. Divisions and distinctions are in a very real way the symptoms of the disease.

Think about it: we are so accustomed to the distinctions in the Church that I wonder if we even stop to ask ourselves why they exist. We've become so comfortable with division and have soft-pedaled it, passing off division as our "doctrinal distinctives" that define our particular persuasion of Christian fellowship. In some cases (very few though, I suspect) these "distinctions" might be acceptable and perhaps helpful, but the tendency is to take these "doctrinal distinctives" and use them as a line of demarcation between right and wrong, between spiritual and unspiritual, between first class and second class Christianity.

In far too many cases, these "distinctives" are used as blaring trumpets to call the faithful to the banner and to dismiss the opposition as ignorant and idiotic simpletons. Worse yet, Christian leaders spout great diatribes condemning certain Christian movements as demonically-induced curses upon the Church. The invective has been absolutely scorching at times, leaving little room for Christian love and unity.

It is this tendency for Christians to attack other Christians that resembles an autoimmune disease.

Don't get me wrong; the Church is called unequivocally to defend the faith against false doctrine and surreptitious teachers of error. This would be a healthy body fighting off corrupting antigens. I'm not speaking of those battles here. I'm speaking of doctrinal distinctives, matters of conscience, and peripheral interpretive matters where good Christian people can differ. When these are used as platforms to attack another Christian or group of Christians, then we have an unnatural immune response in the Body.

HAVE YOU EVER BEEN ATTACKED BY A FELLOW CHRISTIAN OVER A DOCTRINAL DISTINCTIVE?

I asked earlier about your experience with other believers. Have you ever been attacked or accused by another Christian because of some doctrinal distinctive they held in opposition to where they felt you stood? What was your reaction? Were you confused or hurt? Did the accusation feel unnatural or out of place? Would you like to know how the Bible anticipates these situations and instructs us to respond?

Dare I ask if you have ever been on the other side of the equation—the attacker? Perhaps you felt you were approaching a brother in love to correct his wrong thinking or his incorrect Biblical understanding of a matter. Perhaps you had good motives and sincere convictions, but things turned ugly and you found yourself in an argument that really didn't glorify Christ. How did you deal with the fallout? Has there been a breach in fellowship? Would you like to know how to better handle these situations in the future? Would you like to know how to remain in the will of God and show love and grace to your fellow Christian while maintaining your convictions?

Further, have you been to a Christian conference, or do you attend a local church, where other Christian movements have been singled out for ridicule as liberal, compromising, fundamentalist, fanatical, not Spirit-filled, "Holy Rollers," or any other such dismissive and derogatory language? Have you ever heard Calvinists or Armenians being demeaned; liturgical or non-liturgical used as terms of derision; or Pre-tribulationist and Post-tribulationist, tongues-speaking or non-tongues-speaking, immersionist or effusionist, closed or open communionist, KJV-only or NIV-readers, red-carpet or blue-carpet protagonists, or any similar term being used to kindle a flame of division among brothers in Christ?

CARELESS WORDS INVITE DIVISION.

I was at a conference where the keynote speaker (whose name many of you would recognize) very clearly and sarcastically referred to a specific group of Christians as those that follow the Armenian heresy. Wait right there! Heresy is a word not to be thrown around lightly. Paul excommunicated heretics. Would this man say that those who differ with him on these particular issues should be cast out of the Church, handed over to Satan, and denied the fellowship of a shared meal? I don't think Jesus would agree with him. We are sometimes so careless with our words that we invite division. I know from many other sermons I've heard from this man that he has many friends, and he cordially debates with men who hold to the opinion he denounced so strongly. The comment got a hearty chuckle from the crowd who were mostly in agreement with him, but I wonder how many realized that the comment was hurtful to the wider Body of Christ.

On a more personal level, have you ever experienced being shunned by a brother because you didn't agree with his view? Years ago I attended a funeral for the daughter of a very close friend. It was an emotional, difficult funeral for a teenager who had tragically taken her own life. At the gathering after the memorial, a Christian brother engaged me in a conversation about a certain interpretation of the end times. He mentioned a name of someone he disagreed with. Mention is the wrong word: he castigated the man and spewed abuse on his ideas with the invitation to me, "I'm sure you'll agree with me on this." Before his rant could progress further I responded, "Don't be so sure of my agreement with you." I was attempting to slow him down in hopes that he could be more respectful of fellow Christians and engage me in a reasonable discussion. He must have thought that I rejected his view and agreed with the man and the viewpoint he was about to verbally thrash, though, because he completely shut down. Conversation over. Ice and cold wind was all I experienced from that point on.

What do we do with situations like this? How do we rightly view these controversies? What is the mind of God for us when faced with differences among brothers? Are these symptoms of a very deep problem? Can a healthy balance be maintained? Can love, unity, and truth abide in a single Body? Can fellowship across these divides be enjoyed? How do we disagree on particulars while maintaining unity in the spirit and the mission that God calls us to?

These are the questions we are going to work out. Failure to work out these questions will perpetuate the disease. The symptoms are recognizable and the diagnosis plain. The Body of Christ, at least in America, is suffering from an autoimmune disease that is wrecking the witness of Christ to a nation that more than ever needs the Good News of the Gospel. Why am I saying that the Church has an autoimmune disease? Because the diagnosis fits!

Spiritual autoimmune disease, or spiritual mutilation, as I sometimes call it, is what occurs when a member of the Body (a believer) sees another part of the Body (another believer) as an enemy. He then attacks that member, mutilating or destroying an otherwise healthy brother or brothers. In essence, this is the Body attacking itself. It's the disease that causes us to see our brothers and sisters as "so-called" Christians instead of the true and beloved children of God they are.

I have a relative (who will remain unnamed to protect the guilty) who is extremely headstrong, even mule-headed. For some time now, my relative has been experiencing physical symptoms that show something is seriously wrong and his otherwise healthy body is malfunctioning. The symptoms were serious enough to cause any doctor to say, "Seek medical attention immediately!"

In spite of the alarming symptoms, my relative chose to avoid any medical attention for months, due to a great mistrust of the medical establishment. Months of attempted persuasion by loving relatives were to no avail. Finally, a truce was called and a test reluctantly agreed to. But when the test came back positive, "those doctors fixed that test" was the belligerent reply from our obstinate patient; "they tampered with it."

My relative's reaction might be amusing, but the potential health issue is not. Untreated illness, as we all know, often leads to debilitating problems or even death. The importance of timely medical care, diagnosis, and treatment can't be overstated. Denial and avoidance usually exacerbate the problem, regardless of the diagnosis. Once we realize there's a problem, we have the opportunity to seek professional help to identify the problem and get back on the road to health.

My relative didn't trust the system or the doctor, and so attempted to avoid their predicament. We have no such excuse. The system is God's and the doctor is Christ. The diagnosis is trustworthy.

IF THE CHURCH WERE OUR MEDICAL PATIENT, WHAT SYMPTOMS WOULD WE OBSERVE?

If we could put ourselves in the place of the doctor, and the Church were our patient, what symptoms would we observe? We don't have to think hard about that one. The Apostle Paul, perhaps the Lord's greatest medical intern (so to speak), has already covered that ground for us. He does the diagnosing so we, like first year med students, can simply peek over his shoulder to see the notes. The beautiful thing about these notes is that they are Spirit-inspired. The Great Physician Himself wrote them. Paul is simply the messenger. They are reliable, perfectly accurate, immediate, and predictive. They address the Body of Christ in the first century as well as the twenty-first century. What's more, they make a pinpoint diagnosis.

In writing to the Corinthians, it doesn't take Paul long to get to the diagnosis of the disease he sees overcoming that church. He sets the tone of the letter right off. After a short introduction he delivers a stunning revelation.

> I appeal to you, brothers, by the name of our Lord Jesus Christ, that all of you agree and that there be no divisions among you, but that you be united in the same mind and the same judgment.

> For it has been reported to me by Chloe's people that there is quarreling among you, my brothers.

> What I mean is that each one of you says, "I follow Paul," or "I follow Apollos," or "I follow Cephas," or "I follow Christ."

Is Christ divided? Was Paul crucified for you? Or were you baptized in the name of Paul? – 1 Cor. 1:10–13 ESV

Paul wastes no time in reporting what he has heard and what he thinks about it. He identifies the problem quickly, candidly, and I think, with a bit of a sting. I can almost hear Paul's first reaction when he received the news: "Quarreling over teachers? Are you kidding me? None of us are anything—don't they know, it's Christ! Christ is the focus!" He shows his holy exasperation when he asks, "Was Paul crucified for you?" It's unbelievable that they would show such partisanship and division.

Then Paul pleads with them to change course. "I appeal to you brothers, by the name of our Lord Jesus Christ," stop this division and destruction! Get together on this, and work toward reconciliation!

How does this translate to our situation? Would Paul have the same diagnosis and rebuke of the Church today? Consider this modern paraphrase of the same passage:

I appeal to you, brothers, by the name of our Lord Jesus Christ, that all of you agree and that there be no divisions among you, but that you be united in the same mind and the same judgment.

For it has been reported to me by Christianity Today that there is quarreling among you, my brothers.

What I mean is that each one of you says, "I follow John Calvin," or "I follow Martin Luther," or "I follow John Wesley," or "I follow Christ."

Is Christ divided? Was Charles Stanley crucified for you? Or were you baptized in the name of John Piper? – 1 Cor. 1:10–13 TICV

Is there really any difference between what I changed in my Tongue-in-Cheek Version and what Paul wrote to his contemporaries? Would you argue that inserting Luther, Stanley, or John Piper's name is different than Apollos, Cephas, or Paul? Stop and think: Paul either means this, or he doesn't. What he's getting at is critical. Do we have a problem with division and quarrelling in the Church today? According to Paul—according to God—Yes! We can't read this lightly and pass it off as only a first-century issue. This is as contemporary and vital an issue as anything the Church faces.

Some may think this is hyperbole on Paul's part. Does he really expect us to all agree and have no divisions among us? Certainly Paul realizes that arguments and disagreement are part of the human experience. Disagreement and discussion are how we think through issues. It's how we differentiate truth from falsehood. It's how we come to conclusions. It's how we keep the Church pure. Has he forgotten that little falling out he had with Barnabas about John Mark? (see Acts 15). Didn't that end in division and in their going separate ways? So surely Paul must mean something different than what it sounds like on the surface.

IS CHRIST DIVIDED? WAS CHARLES STANLEY CRUCIFIED FOR YOU? OR WERE YOU BAPTIZED IN THE NAME OF JOHN PIPER?

Paul addresses this objection as he finishes the sentence, "but that you be united in the same mind and the same judgment" (See also Rom. 12:16, Phil. 1:27). He really does expect us to be of the same mind, without any divisions. Being united in the same mind and judgment involves cooperative effort. We have to pray, search the scriptures, vigorously debate, seek wise counsel, and entreat the Holy Spirit to guide us into truth. This is a uniting activity. When godly men and women seek God after this fashion, they sow peace and brotherly love, not division. Disagreements may linger, but division must not be the result.

Followers of Jesus are called to unconditional love for one another. We must learn how to preserve unity while enjoying diversity in teachers and nonessential teachings.

Insisting on loving interaction, cooperative truth-seeking, and genuine respect for sincere teachers will eliminate division and spiritual mutilation. When we invest too much confidence in a single teacher, we risk clouding our judgment and creating divisions in the Body. Note chapter 3, verses 1–9, especially verse 7: "So then neither the one who plants nor the one who waters is anything, but God who causes the growth." Paul corrects the Corinthians' teacher-centric error and returns them to the true source of all spiritual activity.

In chapter three, Paul concludes the exhortation he began in chapter one. He says in verses 21–23: "So then let no one boast in men. For all things belong to you, whether Paul or Apollos, or Cephas or the world or life or death or things present or things to come; all things belong to you, and you belong to Christ; and Christ belongs to God." Paul carefully and neatly wraps up all their conceits in men into a fully God-focused conclusion. Christ is our great boast! We are free to shout the glory of Christ in unrestrained praises! We are not free to interrupt the voice of God with strains of man-praise! Brothers! Sisters! Can we listen to Paul on this?

FOLLOWERS OF JESUS ARE CALLED TO LOVE ONE ANOTHER—UNCONDITIONALLY. WHEN WE INVEST TOO MUCH CONFIDENCE IN A SINGLE TEACHER, WE RISK CLOUDING OUR JUDGMENT AND CREATING DIVISIONS IN THE BODY.

It may not surprise you that following after selected teachers wasn't the only symptom of disease in the Corinthian church.

Fast forward to chapter eleven. They didn't divide over teachers alone; there were other divisions and factions. It seems that when they got together to observe the Lord's Supper, they divided up into the "approved" and the "non-approved," so to speak (v. 19). In fact, we could probably make the argument that every chapter in 1 Corinthians discusses some topic that created a faction that their church had split into. These issues served to split the Body into a "first and second class Christian," "spiritual and non-spiritual," "approved and not approved" dysfunctional body. This is just the kind of broken thinking I addressed in my introduction.

Paul doesn't state the reasons why the Corinthians were factious during the Lord's Supper. My guess is that they were factious at all times, and them carrying their divisiveness into the Lord's Supper celebration was an egregious offense to God. This was a deep cut to the Body. To shun a brother in Christ at the very feast that celebrates the sacrifice of Christ and His love toward us! Paul was nearly speechless: "What shall I say to you?" He had no commendation or praise for their different spirituality camps.

Paul concludes by saying in verse 31, "judge yourselves rightly," to contrast the unrighteous judging they were doing in verses 18 and 19, where they were judging one another. Their judging fellow believers as either "approved" and "non-approved" Christians was simply bigotry, and it was wrecking the witness of Christ and ruining the very picture of His victorious sacrifice. Paul warns them at the last, in verse 34, to do certain things "so that you will not come together for judgment." Note how far the heart of man (redeemed men at that!) can sink. To bring an attitude of judgmentalism and condemnation to the very feast that marks our release from God's judgment and condemnation is ungrateful at best. More candidly—it's monstrous. It's a denial of all that the Love Feast represents.

We could go on and point out the many other divisions and factions that may have existed in the Corinthian church. For that matter, we could peruse the New Testament and show the many disagreements, incidents, arguments, personality conflicts, and other issues that are addressed by the apostles. Take the Roman church. Paul addresses the same sort of mindset in Romans 12:16: "Be of the same mind toward one another; do not be haughty in mind, but associate with the lowly. Do not be wise in your own estimation." He repeats this in his prayer for the Roman believers in 15:5-6, ending with the words, "so that with one accord you may with one voice glorify the God and Father of our Lord Jesus Christ." You'll find many other references where Paul exhorts us to single-mindedness: 2 Cor. 13:11, Phil. 1:27, 2:2, Eph. 4:3-6, and Col. 3:12-17 are just a few. In fact, the passage in Ephesians is very sharp. We are commanded there to diligently preserve the unity of the Spirit in the bond of peace. These passages also indicate that this was not just a Corinthian problem. Suffice it to say that we are humanly prone to disagree, exercise pride, create controversy, and get miffed when things don't go our way. Add to this the provocation of the evil one, and we've got a perfect environment for the cancer of pride and judgmentalism to establish itself.

Given that the apostles continue to visit this topic and point out these symptoms, we have an obligation to pay attention, both for our own health and the health of the Body. The symptoms described by Paul point us to the autoimmune disease we have described. They are all indications that something is terribly amiss in the Body. The Body has turned upon itself and is actively destroying otherwise vibrant functions and healthy flesh. The question is this: will we remain in denial, or will we submit to the diagnosis and the treatment plan? Will we be the patient that avoids the doctor at all costs and then sabotages the tests to evade the diagnosis? Will we say to ourselves that the disease is not that big a deal, and ignore it?

A better question might be—is this issue really a problem, anyway? Aren't you making a mountain out of a molehill, Jim? Isn't the Church suffering from nothing worse than a common cold that doesn't cause any permanent damage?

Worthy questions. Minor problems do often resolve themselves without attention—but serious disease rarely does; ignoring cancer will not make it go away. Paul emphasizes unity so much, though, that we have to wonder why it's so important to him.

But Jim, what's at risk? Is it really that big a deal? So what if we have some divisions in the Church—aren't we all still preaching the Gospel, encouraging the saints, winning souls, and in the end, glorifying Christ? Why take so much time on this when there's a world to be won?

Again, worthy questions. Let's get our answer from the Lord Himself.

CHAPTER THREE

WHAT JESUS REALLY WANTS

WE CHRISTIANS SPEAK OFTEN OF the passion of Christ. When we do, we usually mean the entire experience of His humiliation, torture, death, burial, and resurrection. I would like to rewind a bit and focus in on the hours before He was betrayed. There's a passion consuming the mind of Christ that burns itself onto the pages of Scripture. Embers kindled in that same fire glow in some of the passages we've cited and others we have yet to cite. This passion is recorded in John 17, a passage often referred to as the High Priestly Prayer of Christ.

It was after Judas had departed the upper room on his desperate errand, and before Jesus and the disciples entered Gethsemane that Jesus stopped, most likely on the crest of the hill that descends into the Kidron Valley, and prayed. His prayer is the outpouring of His eternal desire and immeasurable affection. It is a window into the great heart of God. It is the crystallization of the intimate thoughts of the Godhead as they communed together on the night before the most horrific schism ever to occur. It is the craving of Christ in the hours before He would be separated from perfect Love and forced to bear alone the sin of the world.

What could the Lord of Glory possibly be thinking at that hour? What burned so brightly in His mind and heart that it burst out for all eternity to read and experience? What were the last words of a Man soon to be murdered by those He had fashioned with His own hands? Are His words important? Are they powerful and life altering? Are they worthy of deep meditation? Some say a man's final words are the most important he ever speaks. What about these final words of the God-Man? Granted, they are not the final words of Christ on earth, but they are the final words of Christ to the Father concerning the Church and spoken in the hearing of the apostles.

Take a few moments to read John chapter 17. Perhaps you have some time to meditate on the passage. What do you hear Jesus praying? What are His impassioned supplications? What is He asking the Father to do?

"... THAT THEY MAY BE ONE EVEN AS WE ARE ONE."

I had a Bible teacher who taught me to look for the action words in Scripture. Verbs are often the key to understanding the point of the passage. They certainly mark out the requests Jesus is making in this prayer. Find the action words and you find the focal points of Christ's prayer.

The first action word is just six words into the prayer, "Father, the hour has come; glorify Your Son." The second action word is the same, in verse 5: "Now, Father, glorify Me." If you look toward the end of the prayer you'll see that Jesus also ends with this request. The prayer is bracketed with Jesus's desire for His and His Father's glory. The entire prayer is permeated with the Savior's excitement over His restored and shared glory.

I don't think we have any way to comprehend the depths of Christ's desire for the restoration of the glory He shared with His Father before the world was. We can read it, but we can probably never know it. We have to realize that Jesus voluntarily submitted Himself to a veiled glory. He veiled Himself with human flesh like that which He designed in concert with the Father before the world began. He left the adoration of saints and angels in the heavenly realms to wear the taunts and abuse of earth-bound rebels who despised Him. How can we understand the pain of this rejection and the stifled anticipation of a return to His rightful exaltation?

Think about it: Jesus shared GLORY with the Father! Glory we cannot describe except to repeat that "our God is a consuming fire." Glory that must be invisible lest we see it and perish. Glory that forcibly prostrated the nation of Israel when it descended on the temple (see 2 Chron. 7:1–3). Shared glory that resounds with goodness and eternal lovingkindness. Glory that binds the Son and the Father and the Spirit. Glory inexpressible with the human tongue, barely explained by the tongues of angels, reserved for the language of God Himself to express in the Holy of Holies. How Jesus craves it, how He deserves it, how He expects it, and how He wishes us to share it! All of this and more are expressed in His pleadings. We should linger here—we should write volumes—we should fill our souls with Christ's glory; sadly, we have to move on. Fortunately, our subject does not wander far from the glory of God. In fact, no worthy subject does. If we could just visit this high thought, this great theme, more often in our churches and private meditations, we might find ourselves humble enough to seek that which He prays for next.

Tracking through the prayer (John ch. 17) we read, in verses 6–10 and 12, Christ's claim to glory. He manifested the Father's name to the Father's own, He told them everything, He caused them to believe by sharing perfect words through a perfect life. He kept them, guarded them, and lost none save the one who determined not to believe. Now He has to part with them. What does He want for them? What does His perfect heart long for in respect to those He loves? Look for the action words.

If anticipation of His own glory is the first set of brackets surrounding the entire prayer, then anticipation of unity for the Church is the second set of brackets within the first. "Holy Father, keep them in your name . . . that they may be one," in verse 11 serves as the first bracket surrounding the body of prayer for the Church. The second bracket is in verse 21, "that they may all be one." These brackets wrap this section of the prayer with the theme of Unity. Hold that thought while we look inside the brackets.

Jesus's first request inside the brackets is that the Father would "keep them from the evil one." Jesus has protected and guarded his disciples in order to preserve them for His own; now He wishes the Father to do the same. Jesus has the future in mind here. He wants his disciples to see something, something they haven't seen in its fullness yet. You'll find it in verse 24. Jesus wants his disciples to see His glory. He wants them to make it all the way through the torn veil to see Him in person at the right hand of God. He knows the devil wants to sift them, to destroy them, to keep them from the joy they will share with Him. He pleads with the Lord of Hosts to protect them from the lord of murder and lies.

Jesus's second request is, "Sanctify them in the truth; Your word is truth." He sanctified Himself so that we might be sanctified. He is the Logos, the Word. He is sanctified and we are sanctified in Him by the will and working of God the Father. Sanctify is a high-sounding word. Some might say a "churchy" word, a holier-than-thou word. But it simply means to be set apart for the desire of God. Jesus wants to set us apart for Himself. He desires us. He desires us to be with Him and to see His glory. Jesus, fountain of love, source of all goodness, hiding place of all the treasures of wisdom and knowledge wants YOU! He wants us to share His likeness and glory so we can share His presence.

It has always been God's desire to dwell with men. Think through the Bible. What did God want to do with Adam? Walk with him in the cool of the evening. What was the purpose of the Tabernacle? So that He could dwell among His people. What was the purpose of the Temple? So that He would have a permanent house among His people. Why did He send Jesus? So that He could draw us to Him, save and sanctify us, and have us forever with Him. Draw that in! Breathe the freshness of that pure air! God wants you. God loves you. God fights for you. God sings over you. God yearns for your company.

Lest we mistakenly think this prayer was for the immediate audience only, Jesus carefully adds what we find in verse 20: "I do not ask on behalf of these alone, but for those also who believe in Me through their word." That would be every believer from Pentecost until the consummation of the age. That would be me, and you that have by grace been saved. Isn't it comforting that Jesus thought to tenderly pray this promise so we wouldn't miss it? I often wonder if Jesus scanned every face of every soul He would save while hanging in agony on the cross. I sometimes imagine that He looked at me across the ages and longed for me. I'm so happy to be captured by Him.

THE UNITY OF THE CHURCH IS THE PROOF THAT GOD THE FATHER SENT GOD THE SON AND THAT GOD THE FATHER LOVES THE WORLD.

Once He includes us all He gets back to the main point of His prayer for the Church: "that they all may be one, even as You, Father, are in Me and I in You, that they also may be in Us." I don't pretend to know anything beyond a distant and vague sense of what might be involved in being one with God. Phrases like this tempt me to mysticism. They befuddle me. They twist my mind in the same way the Trinity does. I probe the barriers of eternity only to find myself tired and vacant, and completely awed. I can and will make an attempt at what it means for the Church to be one, unified for Christ and with one another. But to explore the depths of oneness with Christ and the Father is beyond my capability and the scope of this work.

The request for us all to be one is mystical and intriguing on its own, but Jesus doesn't leave us with that thought. He goes on to mention the why behind His prayer for unity. It's the great why that captivates me and answers the questions we asked at the end of Chapter 2: What's at risk? Is it really that big of a deal?

His prayer could have been merely a nice platitude wrapped in the mystery of Deity for us all to wonder at but never really grasp. It could have been easily read and forgotten due to the impenetrable nature of the subject. It could have been dismissed as God speaking in language too high for us—but Christ did not leave us any of these options. He clearly states the reason He desires unity in the Church. Read slowly with me, verse 21: "that they may all be one . . . SO THAT the world may believe that You sent Me," and verse 22–23, "that they may be one . . . that they may be perfected in unity, SO THAT the world may know that You sent Me, and loved them."

The unity of the Church is THE PROOF to the world that God the Father sent God the Son and that God the Father loves the world. Incredible, that the witness of God to the world hangs on the frayed thread of the unity of the Church!

Think of the ramifications! A unified Church shouts sacrificial love to the world. We are truly an aroma of life unto life when perfected in unity. Expressing accord one with another believer expresses God to lost and dying souls. Unison and harmony sing mighty hymns of compassion and grace, mercy and righteousness, humility and acceptance, to a world blinded by sin and lost in darkness. Let those who have ears to hear—hear! Unity is powerful!

On the other hand, a divided Church is proof to the world that the Father did not send the Son and does not love them. Ouch!

WHEN THE LOST SEE FACTIONS AND FRACTURES IN THE CHURCH, WE ARE SHOWING THEM THAT THERE'S NO REAL JESUS AND NO REAL LOVE.

Strife among brothers is tantamount to denying the Gospel.

It's the devil's holiday to see brothers at odds. It's the world's justification for ignoring and distrusting the Church, the Bible, and God Himself. Brothers, we are (in part) to blame for the continued rejection of Christ. We are culpable in the matter of the message going unheard and unheeded. When the lost see factions and fractures in the Church, they "know" there's no real Jesus and no real love. We need not be surprised at their reaction when we try to tell them differently—our actions are shouting denial, while our words are faltering feints at the truth.

Miserable thoughts, aren't they! What should we do with them?

My will to write about these things is often wrapped tightly in my own guilt for participating in and perpetuating division in the Body. I recoil at the thought of my own failures in this area. I have most likely been one who has placed a stumbling block in the path to peace. Rather than wallow in those thoughts, though, we need to press on. Let's resist the temptation to lie where we've fallen. Let's persevere. Let's strive to see God win this one.

And God fully intends to win. We see this in the return of Christ to His first request and the main theme of the prayer. He wants us to be with Him and to see His Glory. It's all about His glory. Look at how He even ties unity to glory in verse 22. Jesus has given us His glory so that we may be one. The glory, the "otherness" of God, has been given to men, so that we might live in such a way that all men might know that God loves them and sent His Son to die for them. We share the glory of God in order to reflect His character to desperate individuals who are "without hope and without God in the world." We share the unity of God to show the world that there is "One God and Father of All Who is over all and through all and in all." The way we live preaches one thing or the other to the lost—will we "be diligent to preserve the unity of the Spirit in the bond of peace?" (Eph. 4:3).

Jesus ends His prayer with love. He made the Father's name known to us so that we might know the Father's love for Him and for us. I suspect Jesus had in mind that it displays the glory of God to love the unlovely. Jesus came to show that love and to teach us—even to empower us—to love others in the same way. There is so much of the world's destiny hanging on the truths in this prayer. There are heights in this prayer not yet reached by the Church. There are contemplations so vast that we despair to observe even a degree's radius of the landscape. But we must try! We need to get alone with these infinite realities. We need to feel them, to be affected by them, to think God's thoughts after Him, to wrestle with their unlimited power, and finally to bow to their demands. We need to obey. This is personal. This is intimate. This is heart to heart—me and God.

CHAPTER FOUR

"WE HAVE MET THE ENEMY . . ."

AS I WRITE THIS SECTION, I'm tracking the news of several movements of uprisings which are taking place across the world. At this particular juncture of history there are many social outcries against repressive governments, wealthy corporations, unfair policies, unfair distribution of resources, and the like. One fascinating observation for me is that the enemy never seems to be well defined. It's always "them" against "us," with very little discernible definition of who "them" or "us" really is. Once we peel away the rhetoric, the fact is that people are behind the them and the us. People repress other people; people are unfair to other people. It is people who can be greedy, angry, oppressive, merciless, and selfish. The bottom line is, people hurt people.

We are prone to shift blame to entities that escape account-ability. Like these raging debates in contemporary society, some people blame the present problems in the world on big corpora-tions that supposedly suck the life out of people and economies. Some people blame big governments, for exercising policies they see as flawed and preferential to one group over another. Whatever the issue, we can find some big entity to lay the blame to so we do not have to face the consequences of our own decisions. It's the big "them" against the small "us," and we always seem to pull for the underdog.

The problem with this blame game is that those big entities are not seeing, feeling, responsible beings. One cannot hold a corporation or government accountable as a whole—they are simply the administrative organizations at the front of the true reality. They are entities composed of and operated by individu-als—people with the responsibility to make decisions. The entity may have a face, a brand, and a constitution, but its soul is the individuals who see, feel, and act in ways that affect others.

Many Christians see the Church this way. You, too, may have been tempted to blame "The Church" or "Organized Religion" during our discussion of Jesus's prayer in the last chapter. It's the Church, or "Churchians", (as one unbelieving friend of mine calls folks who are dedicated to their local congregation) that are the problem, we often think.

But are we viewing the problem through the wrong lens?

We are blaming an entity that can't do anything as an entity: that is, in the same way a corporation cannot make a decision, neither can the Church. To be precise, the Church is technically a living, breathing spiritual organism—it is the Body of Christ. Practically, though, it cannot, as a whole, make the kind of de-cisions that would render it guilty of the offenses many people pin on it. I've referred to the Church as the entity responsible for the issues we are discussing. Please let me clarify: the Church in this context is responsible only insomuch as it is made up of individual believers making responsible or irresponsible decisions. So there it is: the Church as a whole is off the hook; we are not. Individual believers are responsible to obey Jesus in these matters. To finish the quote from the old Pogo comic strip in the title to this chapter, "Yep, son, we have met the enemy . . . and he is us."

When believers determine to step up to their duty, learn how to behave with each other, and exercise their will toward righteousness, we will see a revolution in the witness of the Church. The loved one I referred to earlier experienced this with their health. They stepped up to their duty to maintain a proper diet, avoid harmful thought patterns, get exercise, and make wise decisions, and they have seen a reversal of the symptoms and a pattern of health for years. They took responsibility, faced down a debilitating disease, and watched their body's natural defenses rise to the battle. Believers need to do the same on the battlefront of spiritual disease. We must engage the fight against aggressive autoimmune disorder. We must stop mutilating one another!

All the Scriptures concerning the correction of this behavior are aimed at our individual hearts. They are addressed to the individual believer's conscience in Christ. As we consider them, I invite you to self-examination. This has to be personal! We cannot read these passages with other people in mind; the finger has to be firmly turned back to our own chest. We have to stand face to face with ourselves in the mirror. We must strive to see ourselves and others as God sees us. Only then can we experience the personal healing and correction that will lead to the healing and harmony of the wider Church.

WHEN INDIVIDUAL BELIEVERS DETERMINE TO STEP UP TO THEIR DUTY, LEARN HOW TO BEHAVE, AND EXERCISE THEIR WILL TO RIGHTEOUSNESS, WE WILL SEE A REVOLUTION IN THE WITNESS OF THE CHURCH.

Let me take the lead and confess a personal fault. I have been guilty of doctrinal snobbery.

What I mean is, I tend to put the battle for the truth of the Scriptures above all other virtues. This passion for truth has led me into many a judgmental attitude and, in too many cases, into action. It has caused me to abandon brotherly love and patience for the false idol of being "right." For those of you who identify with me, please understand that I never want to compromise truth in the name of love. We are commanded to speak the truth in love—but never to forsake one for the other.

My battle is personal. I have to fight my natural bent daily, and constantly submit myself to obey Christ's commands to love my brothers and sisters and to strive for unity with them. The responsibility rests on me. Honestly, it's not easy. I default to a hard stand on the truth (as I perceive it from the Scriptures and orthodox interpretations of them). When something hits my ear that smacks of compromise, I react. I wish I could say that my reaction is always in defense of the name of God, His honor, His veracity, and His character. There are some issues that really beat me up. I'm still asking myself how I'm going to respond when I'm challenged on a couple of these since I'm writing a book on overcoming division and hurt in the Church.

With that confession of personal frailty, I want to turn to the Scriptures. My hope is that we can uncover truth, agree on some foundational principles, and make a loving compromise on what we see differently. My greater hope is that we can all take instruction on how to live with one another amid our differences. There are truths to find. May God help us to submit to them once we find them.

WE ARE COMMANDED TO SPEAK THE TRUTH IN LOVE—
BUT NEVER TO FORSAKE ONE FOR THE OTHER.

The passages addressing our responsibility in the matter of unity are multitude. We will explore a sampling of them. Pay close attention to the reflection of God's desire in these verses. Watch for the character traits of God that empower peace, truth, good will, harmony, love, and cohesion between believers. These passages are representations of how our character must reflect God's, in order to maintain peace and the witness of the Gospel. Let's compare our character with that represented in these instructions. How are we doing? Are we submitted to the Spirit's working in these areas? Have we abandoned our arguments and self-justifications for why we can't obey? This is critical! Remember: Jesus explicitly said that the effectiveness of our Gospel witness to the world is bound to our effectiveness at maintaining unity with our fellow believers.

There are two extended passages on maintaining unity found in Romans and 1 Corinthians. We will devote chapters 6 and 7 to them. They will give us the practical guidelines on how to do what we learn. The passage we'll look at in this chapter is about Christ-likeness, or Holy-Spirit-empowered character. The perfections of God are on display for us here. We are invited to mirror them in Christ. We are incredibly incapable of reflecting them apart from the indwelling Spirit. Let's look at Paul's letter to the Colossians, chapter 3.

> Therefore consider the members of your earthly body as dead to immorality, impurity, passion, evil desire, and greed, which amounts to idolatry. For it is because of these things that the wrath of God will come upon the sons of disobedience, and in them you also once walked, when you were living in them. But now you also, put

them all aside: anger, wrath, malice, slander, and abusive speech from your mouth. Do not lie to one another, since you laid aside the old self with its evil practices, and have put on the new self who is being renewed to a true knowledge according to the image of the One who created him—a renewal in which there is no distinction between Greek and Jew, circumcised and uncircumcised, barbarian, Scythian, slave and freeman, but Christ is all, and in all. So, as those who have been chosen of God, holy and beloved, put on a heart of compassion, kindness, humility, gentleness and patience; bearing with one another, and forgiving each other, whoever has a complaint against anyone; just as the Lord forgave you, so also should you. Beyond all these things put on love, which is the perfect bond of unity. Let the peace of Christ rule in your hearts, to which indeed you were called in one body; and be thankful. Let the word of Christ richly dwell within you, with all wisdom teaching and admonishing one another with psalms and hymns and spiritual songs, singing with thankfulness in your hearts to God. Whatever you do in word or deed, do all in the name of the Lord Jesus, giving thanks through Him to God the Father. – Col. 3:5–17

Paul begins the chapter with, "If you are a Christian then love Jesus and not yourself or the world; in fact, you are dead to yourself and the world, and your only life is in Christ." (My paraphrase.) Based on our death to self and our resurrection in Christ, Paul concludes several things. But before we consider those, can we pause a moment to consider what it means to be dead? Dead people don't do the things they used to. They don't do anything. Paul is using this analogy to point out to us that our old man is dead. We don't do what we used to do. We don't do anything like we used to. Before we died, we lived for our own pleasure, rarely or never considering the desire of our Creator or fellow creatures. Ephesians 1 makes it clear that we were dead, living for the devil, bound to the lusts of our flesh, indulging in fleshly and mental desires, and subject to the wrath of God (Eph. 2:1–3). The passage goes on to paint a very unflattering picture of me without Christ.

That all changed when we believed. Now we live only in Christ. His desire is ours, His will is ours, and His mind is ours. We actually have the ability to live as He lived. We have the opportunity to be filled with all the fullness of God. We can live immersed in the character of God. If I am dead to my former self, then what appealed to me then cannot appeal to me now. What appeals to Christ is what appeals to me now. These are not just platitudes— they are the reality of every Christian who chooses to walk in the Spirit. The fact of being dead to sin is a reality. The process of realizing our deadness to sin goes on until our last breath.

Evidently our deadness is only partial and in process, because Paul tells us to keep killing the earthly parts. In Colossians 3:5–10, he says to kill immorality, impurity, passion, evil desire, greed, anger, wrath, malice, slander, abusive speech, and lying. Do you hear what Paul is saying? The sins he mentions are typically committed against other people and ultimately against God. They are people-hurting-people sins. After mentioning these as attributes and actions of dead people, he goes on to describe and invite us upward to the things living people do.

Living people obey the command to put the old dead things aside, so Paul addresses us as such. "Since you laid aside the old self with its evil practice and have put on the new self" then, in essence, act like this. Before he goes into the attitudes and activities that should be worked into our lives, Paul frames the discussion in language that speaks of unity and the absence of prejudice. These character qualities apply to everyone created in the image of God:

Greek, Jew, circumcised, uncircumcised, barbarian, Scythian, slave, and freeman. I would update this to include any and every other modern description of truly born-again believers. We are to be people who don't see distinctions within the Body. There are no "so-called" Christians among the redeemed.

All Christians are to "put on" a set of qualities that repair the damage made by our former selves. We are to look and act like Jesus in relation to our brothers. Notice how these qualities correct and overcome those Paul described earlier. Those faults were harmful and mutilating to others; these are edifying and peacemaking.

So what are we to put on?

Colossians 3:12–14 is a bulletproof list of supernatural character. It's other-worldly to even consider these qualities existing in anyone on a consistent basis. When a person is clothed in this garb, they are unconquerable. To be clothed in these traits is to be clothed with Christ Himself. Enemies wither when faced with this kind of goodness. Arguments die at the feet of this temperament. We simply can't fight the glory represented here.

This section starts with "put on a heart of . . ." Phrases like this can lose a little impact when translated. It means, in our modern terminology, something like this: "From your deepest inward self produce . . ." and then Paul lists the goodness we are to produce. Drawing from the well of Christ, empowered by the Spirit of God, we are to bring up from the very core of our being the character of God. And it is to look like this:

Compassion: This is the sympathetic understanding and merciful identification that a weak vessel feels for a fellow weak vessel. (See Luke 6:36 and Phil. 2:1.) Simply put, it's the ability to wear someone else's skin; to enter and live in their mind. We are to seek to see through their eyes and then respond with mercy. When used in reference to how God is sympathetic, the Bible uses the word mercy, He is the Father of Mercies. (See Rom. 12:1,

2 Cor. 1:3, James 5:11.) Our hearts should warm to and reach out to brothers and sisters in Christ, whatever their circumstances or beliefs. Mercy for another sinner and identification with them comes from familiarity with our own weakness. When we've drunk deeply from the cup of pain that our own sinfulness has placed in front of us, we can then enter into someone else's painful struggle to help them.

Kindness: This is a saturating, resonant tenderness that brings a determined calm to a needy soul. (See Luke 6:27–36, Rom. 2:4, Eph. 2:4–8.) There are no sharp edges here, no raspy tone. This is heaven-scented help. It's redeeming and selfless. This is commanded of us toward our enemies—how much more toward our brothers!

Humility: This is prostrated service to equally-unworthy beings. (See Acts 20:19, Phil. 2:3, 1 Peter 5:5.) It is heartfelt, intentional recognition of our brother. It is self-erasure. It magnifies Christ by imitating Him. It is a uniquely Christian quality, used by no writer outside the New Testament in a favorable sense. It is giving up our own throne in order to serve others. Humility demonstrates a true and deep faith in God, because it is trusting Him to give us (and our preferences) our rightful place before others—instead of us demanding it from them. As Jesus himself tells us, in His Kingdom the greatest of all his disciples—the most "right" in His eyes—are those who are most humble.

Gentleness: This is mildness or clemency toward another that springs from our own recognition that we deserve the injuries inflicted on us. (See Eph. 4:2, James 3:13, Gal. 6:1, Titus 3:1–3.) Clemency is a word with legal ramifications—it means that we show leniency toward an offender. This is the spirit within a man or woman who appreciates God's mercy because they are able to say to themself, "I deserve death!" They extend that same mercy to others. They say, "I must be gentle with my brother because I am guilty in the same way that he is." It is the quality of someone who recognizes their own weakness and allows it to drive them to pity another's weakness. Interestingly, Peter tells us to defend our faith while being clothed in this attitude (1 Pet. 3:15). Paul instructs Timothy to correct the opposition with this demeanor (2 Tim. 2:24–25). To my shame, it was seldom that I went into a confrontation with my spirit clothed in humility.

Patience: To be patient is to endure indefinite suffering without giving in to passionate outburst (See 1 Cor. 13:4, 1 Thes. 5:14, Heb. 6:15, James 5:8). Patience is commonly directed toward difficult people. It is Jesus suffering the indignities of His trial, abuse, and ultimate murder without rage. He could have vaporized every offender, but He didn't. He humbled Himself unto death, even death on a cross. He patiently endured for the joy set before Him (Heb. 12:1–2). We endure the suffering others cause us for the sake of Jesus.

Tolerance: This is putting up with obnoxious, irritating, often irreverent and obstinate people. (See Matt. 17:17, 2 Cor. 11:19.) The other virtues listed here should instruct us about how we put up with, or tolerate, others. We must put to death all impatience, aggravation, meanness, roughness, impulsiveness (the opposites of the other virtues listed here), and the like, that we might naturally feel towards the person who irritates us.

Forgiveness: This is pleasantly favoring another person with a full pardon. (See 2 Cor. 2:7–10, Eph. 4:32, Col. 2:13.) Forgiveness is wiping the slate clean. It's a gift. Cruelty, unkindness, pride, harshness, impatience, and intolerance die here. Immorality, impurity, passion, evil desire, greed, anger, wrath, malice, slander, and abusive speech are all crucified on this cross. Forgiveness cannot be offered in full when any of these vices are retained. We forgive because God forgave us (Matt. 18:21–35). Note that since we are all of one body, when we forgive one another it is a form of self-forgiveness.

Beyond all these things . . .

Love: This is the divinely unique, unfathomably rich, penetratingly intimate affection called upon to rule all the other graces. (See John 15:13, Rom. 13:10, 1 John 4:28, 1 Cor. 13.) Supernatural love is to infuse and permeate all Christian interactions. It is the binding force of God. It is forged in the furnace of grace by the Holy Spirit, placed as burning coals on the hearth of our souls, and breathed out upon believers and non-believers to warm their affections toward God. It is the all-consuming monarch over everything that is good. It is "the perfect bond of unity."

Volumes could be written on every one of these virtues—volumes have been and should be written on Jesus, who embodies each and every one perfectly. These are necessary traits. These virtues overcome jagged wounds in the Body of Christ. They heal; they mend in ways that are divine and permanent; they carry no temporary balm with momentary relief. They are deeply medicinal, scented with the aroma of eternity. Master these virtues, and peace and unity will be ours (vv. 14–15). Master these virtues and the enemy will no longer be us.

CHAPTER FIVE

THE PICTURE
OF HEALTH

IN JESUS WE HAVE THE perfected picture of the virtues discussed in the previous chapter. He is the picture of spiritual health! His possession and exercise of these virtues is catalogued in Philippians 2. When I think of that chapter, I'm reminded of the Old Testament scribes who were instructed to wipe their pens clean and bathe themselves every time they wrote God's name, Jehovah. I feel like that when approaching Philippians 2: my hands, my computer, my life is not clean enough to consider the purity of Christ manifested here.

Paul means us to think of Christ when we are pondering how to act. The old question, which became a passing fad, "What would Jesus do?", is close to hitting the mark here. I would amend it to say, "What would Jesus have me do?" I'm not Jesus, but I am His, and through the power of the Spirit I can imitate Him. Paul encourages us to do that in this passage.

> Therefore if there is any encouragement in Christ, if there is any consolation of love, if there is any fellowship of the Spirit, if any affection and compassion, make my joy complete by being of the same mind, maintaining the same love, united in spirit, intent on one purpose. Do nothing from selfishness or empty conceit, but with humility of mind regard one another as more important than yourselves; do not merely look out for your own personal interests, but also for the interests of others. Have this attitude in yourselves which was also in Christ Jesus, who, although He existed in the form of God, did not regard equality with God a thing to be grasped, but emptied Himself, taking the form of a bond-servant, and being made in the likeness of men. Being found in appearance as a man, He humbled Himself by becoming obedient to the point of death, even death on a cross. For this reason also, God highly exalted Him, and bestowed on Him the name which is above every name, so that at the name of Jesus EVERY KNEE WILL BOW, of those who are in heaven and on earth and under the earth, and that every tongue will confess that Jesus Christ is Lord, to the glory of God the Father. – Phil. 2:1–11

When Paul says "if" in verse one, we recognize that he is using a device of language that really means "because." Because there is encouragement in Christ, consolation of love, fellowship of Spirit, affection, and compassion, we can enjoy the unity in Christ that Paul is about to encourage. He says since we have these great advantages, "make my joy complete" by exercising them. He then tells us how to get that done. We make Paul's, and God's, joy complete by pursuing harmony. Everything Paul calls us to here has to do with unity.

I am not Jesus, but I am His, and through the power of the Spirit I can imitate Him.

OUR CALL

x   Have the same mind, love, spirit, and purpose as Jesus did. We are on a sheer precipice here. Looking over the edge of this kind of unity makes us dizzy. We can't do justice to the perfect symmetry we're being called to. Paul is pleading with us to think in harmony, love with a single heart, breathe with one breath (or live with one life), and mind the one thing. ONE is ALL. How do we do it? The following gives us a start.

x   Don't be selfish or conceited. The original meaning of selfish was "fascinating." It was used of a person who was electioneering or politicking for office: the kind of person who will say or do anything to get elected or to get what he wants. Conceited is likewise an interesting word in the original. It literally means "vainglory." I.e, seeking recognition or glory for oneself without a good reason, or for empty use. The truth is that none of us has a good reason to seek his own glory, and I can't think of anything positive to say about an insincere politician.

x   Be humble and regard others as more important than yourself. Humility here is the same word Paul cited in Colossians 3. The word regard comes from a word referring to leadership or command. We are to esteem others as more important in the same way that a soldier of low rank esteems or honors an officer of high rank. Duty demands that we freely give our brothers pre-eminence.

x Stop looking out only for yourself, but look out for others' interests also. Paul is entreating us to pay intimate attention to the needs of others. We are invited to look away from our own interests and closely examine what our sister needs. Walk away from your stuff and instead walk toward your brother. Jesus did this. He walked away from glory to tend to us. That's why Paul pleads for us to imitate Him.

x Be likeminded with Christ in these things. This is the same word as in verse two. We are to share the same mind with one another as we share with Christ. We have the mind of Christ, so we must employ it (1 Cor. 2:16). Jesus exercised His will to perfectly coincide with His Father's. He did nothing on His own, but only did that which the Father demanded (John 5:30, John 8:28).

CHRIST'S EXAMPLE

x Jesus never gave up any of His glory or authority. He retained all the perfections of deity while choosing for our sakes to humble Himself. Nothing of His Father's abilities or character was outside His grasp. He did not strive for equality with God—He possessed it.

x While possessing all the power and glory of God, He chose to stoop low enough to serve us. He chose to empty Himself. He stooped lower than a king, lower than a commander, lower than a common man, lower than a paid servant, and became, as it were, a slave. He did no electioneering—He did His Father's will. He could never have won public office. He was far too unpopular in His time and even today. The point is: He willingly became unpopular, servile, and low, even empty, for the good of those whom He came to save. We have to ask ourselves: is our popularity more important to us than our brother's need? Will we submit to slavery for the sake of unity?

x While clothed in splendor far beyond our wildest imagination, Jesus voluntarily put on humanity. He veiled His heavenly beauty by clothing Himself in ordinary, unimpressive flesh. He was paying intimate attention to what our needs were. He looked away and walked away from His own uninterrupted glory in heaven to endure derision and shame. Can we follow Christ and walk away from our own glory? Will we volunteer to share in the suffering of Christ?

x While being the source of life itself, Jesus submitted to death. From Him emanates life, yet Life submitted and died. He did not die honorably like a beloved king, nor as a gallant commander in battle, nor even as a common man of common illness. He died in disgrace and dishonor on a cross, like a thief or a murderer. He chose this for me, for you, and for all who have ears to hear! Paul says we are to "have the same attitude" and make the same choice for your brothers and sisters. Die to yourself and your desires in exchange for intimacy with your Lord and your family, his Church.

x Having obeyed, Jesus now reigns as Sovereign and is "worthy . . . to receive power and riches and wisdom and might and honor and glory and blessing . . . and again . . . blessing and honor and glory and dominion forever and ever" (Rev. 5:12–13). His name is above every name. Everyone will bow to Him! Everyone will confess that He is Lord! And the Father will be glorified! He was deserving of this admiration before He humbled Himself and came—how much more so now! How can we look at His example and retain our pride? How can we meditate on His glory and demand our rights? How can we view perfected unity and then cause division?

Concentrate intensely on these things, my brothers and sisters. Get full of Christ. Beg for the hidden treasures of wisdom and knowledge here. Replicate them. Bless others with them. Glorify God with them. Live and die in the headlong pursuit of these things—it will please God—it will perfect you—it will unify the Church.

We could go on, as there is so much more. We could visit 2 Corinthians 6, and Galatians 5:22, and Titus 3:1–3, Ephesians 4, 1 Thessalonians 5:14–15, 2 Timothy 2:24–26, 1 Peter 3:8, and on and on.

I have to admit, this is a mouthful. To go on might be exhausting. Our senses may be full, our brains a bit rattled by contemplating such high things. We can only take so much. We should probably put our shoes on now and walk a ways in these truths. You may be like me: my mind can only be pressed so far without breaking down into despair when faced with this much grandeur. I want to leave the mountains and walk on flat ground. I want to know how I can possibly put into action such high ideals. I start asking, "How do I do it? Where do I start? How do I maintain it after I start? What does it look like?" and many such questions.

I hope to answer these types of questions in the next two chapters. A quick warning, though: stay with me through both chapters. If you take one and leave the other, you'll miss the complete picture. If you identify with one and forsake the other, you may find yourself unbalanced. Both chapters apply to every Christian on some issue. You may be a "Can" type of person on a particular issue and a "Can't" on another, so you'll need both sets of instructions to properly navigate a peace-making lifestyle.

CAN WE FOLLOW CHRIST AND WALK AWAY FROM OUR OWN GLORY? FROM OUR NEED TO BE RIGHT?

CHAPTER SIX

BEING A "CAN"

IN AT LEAST ONE AREA of my Christian life I started as a "Can", became a "Can't", and stayed there for years, and then became a "Can" again. My experience happens to revolve around one of the most controversial areas of conscience in contemporary American Christianity.

The very fact that I'm taking a position on the topic will probably get me in trouble with the many "Can'ts" that I still fellowship with and dearly love. It's a matter of great offense to the consciences of many precious brothers and sisters. If you are tempted after the next paragraph to write me off as a compromiser, or worldly, or backslidden, please be patient. You may be wondering if you should break fellowship with me. If so, I encourage you to read on, think deeply, and ask if your reactions are in line with God's heart on this or any of the multitude of other matters we face in Christian community. I have no desire to offend you—that would break God's heart and mine. Please remember that I'm using this issue for sake of illustration only, not to open up a controversial topic for discussion. Please know also that I have no axe to grind in choosing this topic. It's simply the one that I am most familiar with in my walk.

The matter of which I speak is music. In my particular circle of Christian friends, music has been and still is one of the most explosive topics of discussion. Books have been written to describe the exact kind of music that is acceptable for Christian listening and what is not. I will not attempt to tackle the arguments for or against this or that genre or application of music here. It has been done expertly on both sides and in abundance. It's an area where good men differ. I might even venture to say it's an area where great men differ, and they differ greatly!

MATTERS OF CONSCIENCE MUST NEVER BE RAISED TO THE LEVEL OF DOCTRINE.

That's an important key. When good men differ, we should be very cautious about becoming dogmatic. In many cases, and I believe in the case of music, preferences are matters of conscience and are not essential Biblical doctrine. One of the difficulties we run into is when matters of conscience are raised to the level of doctrine. Often, when these "doctrines" are not held by another group of Christians, we feel compelled to separate from those brothers and sisters until they come to our point of view. This is a serious problem. The opposite can also happen. An essential Christian doctrine can be reduced to a matter of conscience. When this happens we have another grave difficulty in the Body. I would say that the latter is certainly worse than the former, but not by much. It's often a painful process to reconcile differences on non-essential matters, and it is difficult if not impossible to recover from compromise of essential Christian doctrine.

My journey through the "Can" and "Can't" positions on music went something like this. I came to know Christ as a freshman in college through a campus ministry. My new birth was genuine and radical. I knew instinctively that I was different. I knew that I couldn't do many of the things I used to do, or continue with many of the friends I had. As a new Christian, I started learning and growing. I had a hunger for the Bible. I also had a desire to listen to music that would reflect my new heart. I wanted to hear psalms, and hymns, and spiritual songs sung to me, a desire I had never experienced prior to my conversion.

After getting to know other Christians on campus, I came in contact with music that had a decisively Christian emphasis. I didn't know there were such things as Christian bookstores, but I soon discovered them. I bought all the Christian-themed music I could afford. Groups and artists such as The Second Chapter of Acts, Keith Green, Amy Grant, DeGarmo and Key, The Imperials, and others grabbed my attention (you may be guessing quite accurately how old I am from this list). I was uniquely ministered to by many of the songs. Others were not deeply spiritual, but enjoyable nonetheless. Some, I think, were flippant and not edifying, but they were in the minority. I was blissfully ignorant of any issues with this music: an ignorance that was about to be challenged.

As I progressed in my Christian life I sensed a call toward full time ministry. I believed the Lord wanted me to leave the state university I was in and attend a four-year Bible college. I enrolled in a school that was very conservative in its approach to the Scriptures and to music. The school proudly proclaimed that it was of a specific stripe of Christianity, which I will leave unnamed. I don't want the labels to distract from the point we are exploring. I was attending a church at the time that claimed the same spiritual DNA as the college, and my pastor recommended I go to this school to prepare for the ministry. It was the perfect place for me, and I am forever indebted to the lessons I learned both in and outside the classroom. The Lord used my professors, friends, faculty, and the local churches to mold me in ways I don't think were possible anywhere else.

As I said, this Christian university took and still takes a very specific view on the genres of music acceptable for Christian listening. Without going into detail, acceptable music could be loosely identified as classical and sacred. Classical is in the vein of Bach, Beethoven, Grieg, Handel, Chopin, and similar composers, if they were performed conservatively. Hymns and gospel songs would represent sacred music. Tunes ranging from Bernard of Clairvaux to Ira Sankey and Fanny Crosby, and anything contemporary but maintaining that style, were considered appropriate.

The teaching was that the music I had been listening to in my early walk was not acceptable, was worldly, and was even dangerous to my relationship with Christ. Teachers, church, and the overall atmosphere of the school informed my conscience on the matter. I became convinced of the veracity of the arguments for this view and was a strong proponent of it for at least a decade. I will add that I did not take the time to study the topic firsthand in the Scriptures, but rather accepted uncritically what was taught. I know now that it was a shameful thing for me to form an opinion (especially such a stern one) about things I had not spent any time asking the Lord about!

I was so strong in my opposition to anything outside these genres that I was easily offended when I had to be subjected to other forms of music in stores, or while watching sports on TV, or any other venue. I was offended to the point that if someone claimed to be a Christian and listened to music that I considered off limits, I would write them off as an unbeliever or, at best, a backslidden compromiser. I would literally become angry that I was made to endure their "wicked" music. As long as I stayed in the comfort zone of like-minded friends, I was able to count myself righteous. I was quite convinced of my superior spirituality compared to those others' worldly form of Christianity.

I'm probably even now raising a furrow on some brows that still hold to this view. I am not trying to offend, just illustrating a point by way of a long explanation. Please bear with me.

As I mentioned, my views on this and many other topics have been drastically altered, not by convenience or company, but through lonely toil in the workshop of Bible study. I've spent hours in the Word upon this and many other topics that once held me in unwavering dogmatism. I'm happy to say that I've come full circle through this view and am back to the freedom I had when I first came to know Christ. I enjoy the liberty of listening to many different genres. I marvel at the reflected creativity of our God. It is endless, beautiful, and thrilling. I'm thankful that I can glorify the Lord in ways that I could not in times past. Am I saying that anything goes? Please, I beg you not to fall to the temptation to pin that label on me or any other believer. Every conscience has God-set boundaries. The boundaries concerning non-essentials can and are different for every believer, by God's own design. We will see this clearly in the passages we are about to explore.

EVERY CONSCIENCE HAS GOD-SET BOUNDARIES.

For those of you I have caused to shudder with the personal illustration of my journey and my present position on a controversial issue I beg you—read on. I know some of you are now tense and may be having a hard time seeing me as credible, after my confession. I could have brought up issues such as End Times, Use of Spiritual Gifts, Mode of Baptism, Order of Salvation (Faith, Regeneration, Calling, etc), Remarriage, Female Elders, Church

Government, the Role of Christians in Public Affairs, or any number of controversial Christian issues. If I just stepped on your issue, then we share something in common—it has been one of my issues for nearly thirty years now. I invite you to endure and visit the Scriptures with me to learn just how you and I are to get along, when we disagree so firmly over this or any other subject.

As we stated earlier, it's beautiful that God knew that we would struggle with disagreements. He knew our battles before they were engaged, which ones would cause deadly divides, which ones would ignite flaming rhetoric, which ones would gash the Church so deeply that many would wonder if she could ever recover. All this was anticipated. The Holy Spirit informed the Apostle Paul just how to handle controversy between brothers. He even names the two sides of the equation in terms we might find uncomfortable—stronger and weaker brothers. No one wants to be considered weak, but God very gently uses that term to describe one side of a pressing first-century dilemma.

Let's look at the issue, define it in contemporary terms, and then learn how the stronger brother is to view his role in maintaining unity in the body. In the next chapter we will consider the weaker brother and his role in maintaining Christian accord.

Paul addresses contemporary issues with timeless truths. We find his instructions on dealing with disagreements over matters of conscience in Romans 14–15 and 1 Corinthians 8–9. The issue in the first-century church was whether or not a Christian could eat meat that had been offered to an idol. This concern is not unlike many of our contemporary debates. The ultimate answer for those believers was yes and no. Some could, some couldn't. To some it was sin, to others it was not. Some consciences are bound and some are liberated. This seems like a tangled contradiction, but once we work our way through Paul's arguments, we will see that there are reasonable resolutions for both sides.

I would reproduce the Romans and 1 Corinthians chapters here for you, but space will not allow. So I invite you to have your Bible open to these passages as we follow Paul's instructions to the two parties involved in this dispute.

Paul begins by addressing the Roman Christians with a term that makes me chafe. The first person he mentions is "the one who is weak in faith." He's not speaking to the weak-in-faith person yet, but he is speaking about them. I don't know how that description strikes you, but I personally don't want to be seen as weak. It somehow militates against my sense of who I am. Which, I think, is one of the reasons we have such difficulty coming to terms with disagreement in the Body: we have difficulty seeing our position as the weak position.

A quick aside: When Paul uses the term weak, he is not being derogatory. He is simply describing brothers whose conscience says "no" to certain issues where others can say "yes." They have no less standing before God or in the Body. They are equally loved and nurtured by God. They are accepted in the beloved as enthusiastically as the stronger. They may even be more Biblically literate than the stronger brother. We need these reminders.

PRIDE LOVES A STRONG ME AND A WEAK YOU.

In addition to having difficulty seeing our issues or ourselves as weak, we tend to be very comfortable with identifying others as weak. Do you see how this can aggravate an already difficult situation? This is called pride. Pride loves a strong me and a weak you. Pride is the centurion of the old man who stands guard against the intrusion of true humility in these matters. We have to deal with that. If we are to overcome disagreement and pursue harmony, our pride must die. Paul's approach gives us practical and effective weapons to fight this war.

For the moment, let's be the stronger brother. I call him the "Can". In Paul's example he's the one who can eat anything, whether offered to an idol or not. He's free. He can exercise his liberty in this issue without offending his conscience. His holiness and standing before God are not compromised. It's a position I think we all relish being able to have.

I have to realize, as a stronger brother, that I have an obligation to my weaker brothers. I am bound to behave in specific ways in order to maintain the unity of the Church. Before we get to our list of detailed orders, let's update the argument. We don't wrestle with meat offered to idols today, at least not in our modern Western culture. Our issues are different in substance but not necessarily different in application. If we were to list all the contemporary issues that are subject to the guidelines Paul is laying down here, I'm sure it would be intolerably long. We do need to define some key distinctions though.

What sorts of issues is Paul addressing? Is he addressing merely issues of preference, or matters of conscience, or does he include doctrinal matters as well? Are we to apply these instructions to doctrinal disputes in the Body? Are they just for "peripheral" Biblical issues that are subject to varying interpretations? Or are they restricted strictly to matters of conscience? Let's define our terms.

x   Matters of Conscience—These are issues that are not dogmatically or specifically addressed in Scripture. Examples include but are not limited to: May I smoke a pipe? May I sit in a bar and have a beer with a friend? May I go to a movie theater? May I listen to secular or contemporary Christian radio? How should a Christian woman dress? To be clear, there are Bible principles that apply to each of these issues, but there are no black-and-white guidelines, prohibitions, or detailed instructions giving us crystal clear truth that eliminates all disagreement.

x   Doctrinal Distinctives—These are issues specifically mentioned in Scripture, but that are still open to legitimate differences in interpretation. These are considered Bible doctrine or they touch on doctrinal matters, but do not rise to the level of Essential Christian Doctrine. These issues include: What is the proper mode of baptism? How often should we take communion? What is the preferred structure for local church government? Which Bible translation is most accurate? How do we worship God in public assembly? Are the miraculous gifts still in use? What day is best to meet for worship? Can someone lose their salvation? What is the correct interpretation of End Times passages? We could go on. If I missed your favorite, please forgive me.

x   Essential Christian Doctrine—This is the short list of absolutes that define Christianity. Without believing these, one cannot be considered Christian. They are clearly defined and are not open to differences in interpretation. Clear moral absolutes can be placed in this category as well. There are some disagreements about the doctrines that are necessary to include here, but the historical Church has come to relatively solid agreement on the essential core. We will list these in a subsequent chapter.

These definitions can be muddied. Some elevate matters of conscience to the level of doctrinal distinctive or even essential Christian doctrine. Some elevate doctrinal distinctives to the level of essential Christian doctrine. Or the reverse: some consider essential Bible doctrine to be debatable, or worse, a matter of conscience. Where do we draw the line? What exactly is Paul getting at with these instructions? Do they cover one or all three of these categories? As we work our way into the chapter we will answer these questions.

Sitting at Paul's feet, so to speak, while he teaches on this topic is revealing to me. I'm seeing a tender yet firm hand in his approach. There's mercy mixed with celebration. He celebrates the freedom we have in Christ while warning us not to abuse it. He begs us not to hurt one another.

Paul's first command reflects the approach. His command to the strong is to accept or welcome the weak. The word command may seem over the top, but I don't think so. How do we view Bible instruction: as mere suggestion, or as our absolute duty? If our absolute duty, then Paul is giving us commands and not simple suggestions. We have to read this teaching as the Lord's expectation for our behavior.

Paul's first command is that we are to welcome weaker brothers. Thayer's Greek Lexicon unveils the core reality beneath the command by defining the root word as "to grant one access to one's heart."[2] Access to our heart is not the first thing we think of giving to someone who is challenging our positions or is offended by our freedom. Paul goes on to say that we welcome them without passing judgment on them. Rutherford, in his translation of Romans says, "Although in his faith a man shows weakness, I bid you welcome him to your society without desiring to contest his opinions."[3] In other words, we are to grant them access to our hearts without regard to their convictions about disputed matters. That's a massive statement!

---

2   A Greek-English Lexicon of the New Testament, Joseph Henry Thayer (Grand Rapids, MI: Zondervan, 1956), 139.

3   Saint Paul's Epistle to the Romans: A New Translation with a Brief Analysis, William Gunion Rutherford (London: Macmillan, 1900), accessed on Google Play, 59.

"... WELCOME HIM TO YOUR SOCIETY WITHOUT DESIRING TO CONTEST HIS OPINIONS."

We see here that it is our temptation to pass judgment on weaker-in-faith brothers. Judgment usually doesn't get passed from a position of humility; self-righteous people are the ones who tend to unfairly judge others. Another temptation for those strong in faith is named in verse 3: "The one who eats [the "Can" brother] is not to regard with contempt the one who does not eat." The temptation is to despise (yes, the word is that tough) those who limit our liberty. Isn't it true! Don't we feel the tide of disdain rise in our minds when someone casts an upturned brow in our direction? Our natural response is a visceral reaction when we sense we are being judged. But Paul directs us to respond opposite to our natural tendency. We are to respond supernaturally. We are to resist the desire to see fellow believers as less than Christian.

The next logical question is, "How do we do that? How do we quell that rising emotion and turn it to love for our brother?" There are actually twenty items in the Romans 14–15 passage instructing the "Cans" on how to do it. I'll list them alongside the verses and include some short comments to shine light on how they might work in daily application.

x Welcome those with issues of conscience (v. 1). We covered this one but, to summarize, we open the door to our heart without challenging their conscience.

How do we apply this? I heard an anecdotal story that illustrates this in real life. A church body, which practices exuberant worship through contemporary music, invited a well-known preacher to come for a preaching conference. The preacher was from a musically traditional background and had often taught about the dangers of allowing contemporary music into the Church. How do you suppose he responded to the invitation? Perhaps to our surprise, he accepted, with one caveat. He asked the inviting church if they would be willing to just do hymns while he was there. He didn't want to offend his conscience and at the same time he didn't judge their liberty. Beautiful, I think! How do you think the inviting church responded? They accepted, prepared to worship with hymns, and enjoyed a God-blessed conference. This, brothers, is the way things ought to be in the Body! Peace within difference is not impossible to maintain.

How do we do it personally? I know many Christians who differ with me on many different topics. Some of them are matters in which I have great liberty and they have none. With those brothers, I remain silent on the topic of my liberty. If they visit my home, I put away anything that would offend their conscience: it might be an NIV Bible, it might be a music CD, it might be a movie. Why be careless, and so provoke their conscience and risk an argument? This is a simple and uneventful practice of mine. It keeps peace and warm fellowship between brothers. I don't chafe at being scrutinized—I scrutinize myself in light of my brother's visit, so he is free to enjoy our time together.

x   Don't attempt to persuade them contrary to their conscience: "not to quarrel over opinions" (v. 1). This is enormous! This one stops us in our tracks. We are not permitted to argue with this brother or try to convince him to change his mind. This probably solves 98% of the arguments we have with fellow Christians! If we are at peace with the idea that we don't have to correct them, so they can be "right" or "free," we will have a much easier time living in harmony. God is the author of their conscience. He will work with them in His time. Don't engage the argument.

Let's test our hearing. The Scripture says: Do Not attempt to persuade them contrary to their conscience. Isn't that remarkable! Can you hear that? But shouldn't we try to free them up? The simple answer is, no. The natural question that knocks on the door of my mind is, "What if they bring it up?" Great question. Doesn't it seem that those who are offended by my freedom are the first to address the issue? That resonates with my experience. They want me to "handle not, touch not, taste not." How do we address those conversations? We'll discuss it in the next chapter.

Practical application of this one is easy. Keep your mouth shut about their issues of conscience. Steer the conversation away from them.

PROPER ATTITUDES TOWARD OUR BROTHERS AND SISTERS ARE FORGED IN THE MILLS OF HUMILITY BEFORE THE THRONE OF GOD.

x Don't despise those who can't participate (v. 3). Don't be angry with them for limiting your liberty. Rather, help them and be patient with them. (See also Acts 20:35, 1 Cor. 9:22, 1 Thes. 5:14). This demands that we clothe ourselves in the character we covered in chapter 5; we must put on this suit!

Application of this one happens in the quiet recesses of our hearts before God. It takes place in our prayer closet and personal Bible study. It happens when we daily abandon ourselves to the Spirit. We can't expect to resist this temptation on the spot; we have to prepare for it. Proper attitudes toward our brothers are forged in the mills of humility before the throne of God.

x Be fully convinced (of your convictions) in your own mind (v. 5). Know where you stand, and stand there in confident humility. Rejoice when your Bible-trained conscience does not condemn you. Resist the temptation to be smug in your satisfaction. This means study your Bible—get the mind and heart of Jesus on the issues. The Bible must instruct your conscience! If you are not chasing truth like you were on fire, then you are doing yourself and your fellow believers a great disservice—not to mention storing up rebuke from your Father. End your empty pursuits and get in the Word!

x Honor the Lord with your liberty (v. 6). Exercise your liberty for God's honor and glory, not for your own pleasure. Live out your conscience to His resounding praise. Ours is an exuberant slavery.

Peter was introduced to liberty in the vision of the animals in Acts 10. Not only did Peter learn that God shows no favoritism, but he learned that God had also declared all foods clean. That was some kind of shocker to Peter! My freedom shocks me at times. I'm in awe of the goodness of God, and that He wants me to be utterly filled . . . with joy in Him. Turn your freedom into energetic, grateful praise. Allow your heart to be filled to bursting: this will honor God!

x Give thanks to the Lord in your liberty (v. 6). Be thankful in everything—especially the freedom we have from sin and unto grace.

J. R. MacDuff said, "Cultivate a thankful spirit! It will be to thee a perpetual feast."[4] The daily practice of thanksgiving will cultivate humility, love, kindness, open-eyed wonder, and gentleness toward God and man; make it your habit to go out of your way to say thanks!

4   *Record of Christian Work, Volume XXXV*, Edited by W. R. Moody (East Northfield, MA: Record of Christian Work Company, 1916), 167.

x Don't live selfishly (v. 7). Recognize that you are not an island. The strong have an obligation to the weak. Community cannot contain conceit!

MY FREEDOM IN CHRIST SHOCKS ME AT TIMES.

Do you know of churches or groups of Christians that keep to themselves? Churches in which, if you are not a part of their fellowship, you are not welcome? I once lived near a church like this. It was a small group led by a stern man. I attended a prayer meeting there once. I have to admit that the reception was distant and frosty. I got the distinct impression that the congregation wanted to be friendly but didn't know if it was "approved" to offer me a welcome. I got to know a few of the members of that congregation over time and learned that my first impression was the right one. They truly did have to be careful who they fellowshipped with, or else they would face the ire of their pastor. They grieved that they could not offer me open-armed fellowship because they feared what the leadership of their church would say. It was a sad experience, and one that is completely foreign to the loving acceptance we are instructed to show to all believers in Christ. (See 3 John 9–10 for an apostolic rebuke of this type of behavior.)

x Recognize your ownership: you are a slave of Christ (v. 8). As slaves, we should be quick to respond to our Master's desires, and His clearly stated desire in John 17 is the unity of all believers. Pursue it!

x Remember that Christ died and rose that He might be Lord! (v. 9). Whether we live or die we belong to Him. Make that your comfort; rest there. Drop the insistence that you be "right" and focus on the main thing—you are loved by Jesus. Daily restore to Him the dominion over your doings. Set Him up as King, moment by moment. Crucify those parts of you that seek to ascend to Christ's throne. Starve them, kill them, and shrivel them with the Light of God's Word.

x   Remember that Christ will judge your actions and attitudes (vv. 10–12). This is sobering. It will look something like John 21. Imagine Peter's inner turmoil as Jesus examined him. The naked feeling of total exposure will be devastating if we choose to disregard these commands.

The judgment you may be receiving from a weaker brother is painful. You can endure this pain. If we choose to react to their judgment and mistreat our weaker brother, we will have to endure the judgment of Christ for wounding His Bride. Hearing His disappointment will be intensely painful—much more so than the pain we feel now at the slight of our brother. Getting to the place of cherishing His smile above any earth-bound approval will lift us beyond the difficulty of being misunderstood by our brothers.

x   Don't put a stumbling block in the way of a brother (v. 13). Stop judging in matters of faith and conscience. Accusation is painful even if it's false; it's doubly painful when it's true. Can any brother bring a charge against us for tripping him in his weakness? Have we offended? Have we violated God's chosen lambs? Have we wrecked the witness of the Church? Abandon your need to set your brothers right on questions where good men debate and differ. See the suggestions under #1 for this one as well.

BELIEVERS HAVE DIFFERENT BOUNDARIES BEFORE THE LORD. SELF-DISCIPLINE FOR THE SAKE OF A BROTHER OR SISTER IS A HALLMARK OF A MATURE BELIEVER.

x   Acknowledge for yourself that nothing is unclean, while acknowledging that something may be unclean to a weaker brother (v. 14). This is not a license for moral evil. This is an acknowledgment that believers have different boundaries before the Lord. I can, you can't. I have permission in my spirit, you do not. I don't sin in a matter, you do. Can we hear these statements and accept them? Even if we cannot comprehend them, will we apprehend them and make them ours? Will we accept them as God's design and fully submit to God's truth? Will we love the "Can'ts"?

x Do not grieve your brother (v. 15). If you do, you are not walking in love. 1 John explodes this into burning reality. According to John, not walking in love with our brothers and sisters may be proof that we don't even belong to the Lord. That hurts. Don't let your exercise of liberty cause others to doubt if you are born again. Grieving your brother for selfish indulgence is a tragedy. The formula for unity here is Abstinence = Love. Meditate deeply on 1 John for this one—get John's words under your skin. Bathe your heart in this truth—check your salvation in the mirror of your love for your brothers.

x Don't destroy the one for whom Christ died (v. 15). Better a millstone hung about our neck, causing us to sink to the depths, than that we should offend His little ones. Have pity! Stoop to help your brother. Better yet, don't entertain the thought that you are stooping. You are reaching across to a fellow helpless saint, hoping that you may both one day be saved.

x Don't let your good (exercise of liberty) be seen as evil (v. 16). Limit your liberty for the sake of the Lord and His good name. Self-discipline for the sake of a brother is a hallmark of a mature believer. Wash your brother's feet in this way. Refresh his spirit by putting aside your freedom.

x   Recognize that the kingdom of God does not revolve
around your liberty (v. 17). You are bound to Christ and
must obey His directives for Body unity.

**THERE MUST BE NO PRIMA DONNAS IN THE CHURCH—THE
GREATEST WILL BE SERVANTS, NOT SPOTLIGHT CRAVERS.**

x   Seek righteousness, peace, and joy in the Spirit (v. 17).
These lead to harmony. These carry the aroma of unity.
We should have agreement in this quest.

x   Rejoice that you are acceptable to God and approved by
men when you limit your liberty in love (v. 18). We all long
for inclusion, approval, and acceptance; here it is. Do these
things and these elusive expressions of love are yours. In
this case, Self-Limited Liberty = Love.

x   Realize that it is good to limit your liberty (v. 21). Limit
your liberty and be one who does good! Live out Galatians
5:13, "For you were called to freedom, brethren; only do not
turn your freedom into an opportunity for the flesh, but
through love serve one another." This is the equivalent of
the "taunting" penalty in American professional football.
We are not allowed to score a touchdown and then display
utter contempt for the other players. Christians are not
allowed to flaunt their liberty in disrespect of God and
their brothers and sisters. Taunting someone else is ugly
and low behavior, and does not at all reflect the dignity of
a child of the King. We are not better than our brother—
just different.

x   Keep a clean conscience—it's between you and God (v.
22). It is literally a thrill to be free from condemnation.
No guilt. No shame. No hiding. No painful anticipation
of God's displeasure. Do you know that feeling? Do you

know that freedom? It's happiness that runs deep. It fully satisfies. Guard it!

There they are. The strong man's twenty. Twenty attitudes and actions that glorify God by maintaining unity. Twenty attitudes that help us minister to our weaker-in-faith brothers. Twenty characteristics that can be summarized with one word—deference. We defer to the glory of God and the good of our brother.

1 Corinthians 8 repeats and expands on these thoughts. Paul makes sure to remind the Corinthians that knowledge tends to create arrogance in those who possess it. He is warning the "Cans" that their knowledge and freedom should not become expressions of pride. Remember that they were fond of teachers and had broken into factions around different teachers. The pride they showed was in their knowledge. Paul says in no uncertain terms, "you really don't know anything as you ought to know" (v. 2). Paul says that, instead of bragging about our knowledge, we are rather to "love God!"

Paul then tells us why the weak brother has a weak conscience. Paul says there are no such things as idols because there are no other gods. There is One God, the Father, and One Lord, Jesus Christ. The reason the brother is weak is because he doesn't know this; his knowledge of the nature of God is incomplete; he still thinks like a pagan in many ways. Therefore, when our weak brother eats meat offered to idols, he thinks the offering was real. We know it's not, but he doesn't. Paul asks us not to offend him. If we do, Paul calls it a sin against Christ.

Paul goes on to say in that letter that we have the right (to exercise our freedom). We Westerners are so concerned about our rights, and we often demand them. Paul in essence says, "Sure, I have rights. I can exercise a lot of Christian liberty rights—but I won't! Not if it threatens my brother's conscience! In fact, I'll stop eating meat for the rest of my life if it benefits my brother." That's the conviction of an unselfish man. Are we willing to completely abandon something we have perfect freedom to do, in order to show love to our brother? What if it's something we really like doing? What if it's one of our top three activities under the sun? What if it's our number one enjoyment? What a challenge!

Let's make a distinction here. We are not talking about those who will legalistically steal your liberty to satisfy their prideful disposition and add another coat of white paint to their sepulcher. We are talking about brothers who have genuine issues of conscience. Brothers who will be spiritually harmed if we exercise our liberty. Limiting our freedoms to satisfy a spiritual snob is exactly what Paul warns us not to do in Galatians and Colossians.

ARE WE WILLING TO COMPLETELY ABANDON SOMETHING WE HAVE PERFECT FREEDOM TO DO, IN ORDER TO SHOW LOVE TO OUR BROTHER? JESUS DID.

Getting back to the text, Paul sums up his attitude in chapter 9, verse 19: "For though I am free from all men, I have made myself a slave to all, so that I may win more." Notice also in verse 22 he even says, "To the weak I became weak." Just as Christ bowed Himself to take on human flesh and attired Himself in weakness to win weaklings, Paul imitates his Master.

The primary issue under discussion has been the eating of meat offered to idols, which we would define as a matter of conscience. But did you notice that Paul addressed another controversy in this context? It's in the Romans passage, chapter 14, verse 5. There Paul slips in a discussion about the observation of days. We understand this to mean that some Roman Christians, especially born-again Jews, may have been arguing over which day to meet for worship: Sunday, or Saturday, or every day. The doctrine of Sabbath observance goes all the way back to Creation—before Christ, before the Law—but there was a great disagreement over which day to celebrate now that Christ had risen. Which day now really constitutes the Sabbath?

Paul says it's up to us, as long as we do it unto the Lord. We would call this issue a doctrinal distinctive: a difference that is clearly a Biblical doctrine but doesn't rise to the level of essential Christian doctrine. Even today there are Messianic Jewish and other congregations that keep the Sabbath on Saturday rather than Sunday, so this remains a contemporary issue. This leads to the answer for the questions we asked earlier: "Where do we draw the line? What exactly is Paul getting at with these instructions? Do they cover one, or all three, of these categories?"

The answer is that these instructions cover at least the first two categories. Paul makes no mention of essential Christian doctrine here. It would be hard to make a case for deciding essential doctrines based on the weaker/stronger mandates presented here. We are not testing doctrine here. We are enjoining deference. Essential doctrine is not subject to personal conscience or variable interpretations. We can be sure, though, that these guidelines are trustworthy for maintaining unity where matters of conscience and doctrinal distinctives are concerned.

Being the stronger brother has been a relatively easy exercise. We are typically pretty good at seeing ourselves in this light. Paul wraps up the admonitions to the stronger brothers by repeating his call to unselfish service in Romans chapter 15, verses 1–3. We are to bear the weaker brothers' burdens, which simply means that we are to practice those twenty things Paul laid out for us. We are to follow the example of Christ in this self-sacrifice.

But what about the weaker brother? What's his obligation? Does he have any responsibility to maintain unity, or does he have no obligations, because he is weak?

CHAPTER SEVEN

BEING A "CAN'T"

DEPENDING ON THE TOPIC OF discussion, we could all fall into the category of a "Can't": a weaker brother. I have some "Can'ts" in my life; don't you?

What makes us a "Can't"? Here it is: if our Bible-trained conscience forbids us to participate in activities that are not specifically condemned as sinful in Scripture, then we can consider ourselves the secondary addressees of this passage: a weaker-in-faith believer. In other words, a believer who has limited liberty due to conscience. This is not a derogatory term—it's a divinely-inspired description of every true believer at some point in their walk with God. God has accepted BOTH "Can" and "Can't" believers—with no distinction.

I'm certain that if we could make a list of every matter of conscience and every doctrinal distinctive that exists in the entire

Church, we would all find one or more that disturb us. There are things not specifically forbidden in Scripture and that many Christians practice, but that we could never agree to. Some of them may fire us up to the point of anger.

How do we respond when we are the "Can'ts"?

I don't respond like I used to!

I hope you haven't made mistakes like I have. I had a very good friend whom I met right after I trusted Christ. He and I became fast companions in Bible study, discipleship, and fellowship. We spent a lot of time together. I've often described him like Jesus described Thomas, "a guileless fellow." He had one of the sweetest temperaments of anyone I've ever known. He had a ready laugh, an infectious smile, and an inability to say anything derogatory about anyone. He was a true joy to be around, and I couldn't have asked for a better brother during the first years of my new relationship with Christ. We had an unbreakable friendship—until I broke it.

About two years into my walk with Christ, I began fellowshipping with some other believers. In the process of getting to know one another, we did what most Christians do: we shared our experience of coming to know Jesus, what church or group we fellowshipped with, what we believed about certain issues, etc. During this discovery period, I felt a bit of tension whenever I would tell these folks about the fellowship I was part of prior to meeting them. Eventually it came out that they believed that nearly everything about my experience as a Christian up till meeting them was all wrong.

Some of these believers described the group I had been part of as "liberal" and "unbiblical." Some of my former practices were called "worldly" and "compromising." And I bought it. My conscience was soon molded by these new "truths" and I could no longer enjoy some of the liberties I once had. I became the weaker brother on many issues I had not previously even thought about. I left the fellowship I had been a part of and I left my friend, without a word of explanation. Not only did I jump on the new bandwagon, I decided I needed to reach out and rescue my buddy from the error he was a part of. You might guess how I exercised my new "truth." I was caustic. I hammered him to get him to see the issues. I sent him pamphlets, wrote letters, called, and even drove an hour and a half to his house once to "remove the mote in his eye." When he didn't get it, I broke fellowship with him. How tragic! I alienated a good brother because I didn't know how to handle differences in the Body from the "Can't" position. My hope is that the following instructions will keep you from making the same mistakes.

ACCEPT YOUR GOD-GIVEN LIMITATIONS, AND DON'T CONDEMN SOMEONE WHO HAS LIBERTY IN AN AREA THAT YOU DON'T.

I spent a good deal of time developing the points in Romans 14–15 and 1 Corinthians 8–9 in the last chapter, so I won't repeat them. Let's dive right into the points of instruction for those who have faith weaknesses on particular issues. I challenge you to get your strongest "Can't" in mind. What is it that enflames you when you see other Christians participating in it? What activities or beliefs bring out that visceral response in you? It is exactly that issue that we should have in mind when considering our duty here. Like the instructions to the "Cans", the instructions to the "Cant's" are also drawn from Romans 14-15.

x If you can't—don't! (Rom. 14:2). Daniel couldn't—so he didn't (Dan. 1:8); Peter couldn't—so he wouldn't, until the Lord Himself corrected him on the issue (Acts 10:14). Accept your God-given limitations in a spirit of thanksgiving. When the Lord desires to release you from a matter of conscience, He will be faithful to bring it about, as in the case of Peter.

x   Don't judge those who can participate (v. 3). Realize that God accepts them. The great temptation of those who can't is to judge those who can. The Christian who does not partake of an activity due to conscience is tempted to condemn the one who has liberty. He sees him as a violator, unholy, and flippant with God's requirements. If we fall to that temptation, we may fall to others such as we find in James 4:11–12, and our speech will become sharp and evil. I've heard speech like this from some of our most admired and well-known Christian leaders. Christian conferences of all stripes are often platforms for incendiary accusations such as these. James says when we speak evil of and judge a brother, we become judges of the Law. Are any of us qualified to scrutinize the commandments of the Lord of Hosts? Justice emanates from Him—who are we to inspect our brothers' motes? We will stand, without excuse, for damage done to the Body by our hell-enflamed tongues. Brothers and sisters, please draw back from this world of iniquity. Speak the truth in love.

I embraced an admonition from my pastor when I was in college. He encouraged us to keep Sunday separate and special. He encouraged us to use the day for rest and meditation. He was very persuasive in his teaching on this, so much so that I think most of the folks in the congregation abided by it. Some adhered in a very legalistic way, and I was one of them.

At the time, I was travelling on Saturdays to a town a few hours from campus to take part in youth ministry with a buddy. We would always stay over at my friend's future in-laws' house, and minister at the Sunday morning and evening services. In between the services, we would eat with the family and he would then melt into the couch with his future father-in-law to watch football all afternoon. I would retire to the guest room to read and rest. I was firm in my resolution to follow my pastor's advice, but my buddy had no such conviction. To his credit, he never tried to coerce me to change my mind, even though he knew how much I enjoyed football.

I had a harder time of it. I never confronted him on his Sunday habits, but I certainly entertained the thought that he was flippant with the Lord's Day, and I wondered how deep his spirituality was. Even as I was doing the right thing for me, I was harboring a "second-class Christian" designation toward him. I was judging him in his liberty. Thankfully and by God's grace alone, I never said anything, or I might have tempted him to despise my rigid conscience on the matter. Thinking back on his display of Christian character is warming to my heart even today. He was a blessed brother to allow me the freedom not to participate.

x   Realize that you don't have the right to judge Christ's slave (v. 4). They stand and fall before Christ—not before you. This is the Corinthian error, breaking up into factions and subsets of "approved" and "unapproved" brothers. The "approved" group judging the "unapproved" and vice versa. Can you stand before Jesus, point to one of His servants, and say, "Jesus, I can't believe you don't punish them for their license. If you knew what you were doing, you would correct that immediately." Preposterous! But it happens every day. Will you be the one to put a stop to it in your own heart and in your sphere of influence? (See also Galatians 5.)

x   Realize that God will uphold the very one you are judging (v. 4). I love the phrase, "for the Lord is able to make him stand." It's very comforting. It keeps me from feeling shame and guilt when someone judges me. If my heart is right with God, your arrows cannot pierce, and no matter how I aim for your heart with my shots, they deflect off this shield. Why are we shooting arrows anyway? Do we really want the responsibility of a judge? Do we want to put ourselves in the place of condemning someone whom God has approved? Jude 24 should arrest our unruly tongues. God is the One who makes our brothers and sisters faultless—not our possibly well-intentioned but petty corrections.

GOD IS THE ONE WHO MAKES OUR BROTHERS AND SISTERS FAULTLESS—NOT OUR POSSIBLY WELL-INTENTIONED BUT PETTY CORRECTIONS.

Before being accused of aiding and abetting (what we know as "enabling behavior"), let me state that we are called to "judge righteous judgment" (John 7:24). Which is to say, call sinful behavior sinful and treat it accordingly. When I say sinful behavior, I'm speaking of clear breaches of God's moral law and intentional aberrant teaching. As Christian brothers and sisters, we are clearly called to hold one another accountable for sin and false teaching, to lovingly correct, and then to patiently and humbly restore the guilty party. Remember that the context of this passage is concerning brothers who have liberty in a matter that you don't. If the issue is not plainly condemned and called sin in Scripture, then you are forbidden to judge.

x   Be convinced in your own mind (v. 5). Don't offend your own conscience. This is a conundrum, isn't it? If we are so sure in our minds that this activity is forbidden, then why can't everybody else see it? Have you ever wondered that? How can God tell me to be convinced, but then forbid me from trying to convince others? That's one of the very sweet things about our Heavenly Father. He is a Father! He fathers every one of His children according to their individual need and their level of maturity. You need things

I don't. I have issues you can't understand. My baggage is mine and I bear it in company with Jesus. As my brother or sister, you are invited to help me bear these burdens, as I am with yours, but ultimately our Heavenly Father has each of our hearts in His hands. My convictions may not even register on your radar—they may seem utterly foolish to you—but not to my Father! I hope this melts you a little, my friend. Your tender, patient, compassionate Abba has an unyielding desire to meet you at the point of your need—your issues don't surprise Him—He sees them and loves you in them and in spite of them. That's worth a smile, isn't it?

x Honor the Lord with your convictions (v. 6). Have you weighed your convictions in the scales of God lately? How does He see your observance of days and your keeping of principles of conscience? Are these principles His, or are they yours? Can we examine ourselves here? Are we holding to convictions that belong to someone else, or did we arrive at them from our own arduous labor in the Word? I wish I had a dollar for everyone who has challenged me on a conviction they could not support from Scripture by saying, "I don't know the particulars because I'm not a Bible scholar, but you should talk to So-and-so." I appeal to you, brothers and sisters—don't let "expert" opinions cloud your pure understanding of God's Word. Don't adopt someone else's convictions as your own, unless you are fully convinced from your own fellowship with God in the Word. This is not to say we shouldn't submit ourselves to godly teachers when God has clearly called us to be under their teaching. It is to say that no man's teaching is beyond scrutiny, and our conscience is to be bound to

Christ—not to any teacher. Paul made this very clear in 1 Corinthians, chapters 1–4.

NO MAN'S TEACHING IS BEYOND SCRUTINY, AND OUR CONSCIENCE IS TO BE BOUND TO CHRIST—NOT TO ANY TEACHER.

x   Give thanks to the Lord for your convictions (v. 6). Every good gift and every perfect gift comes down from the Father of Lights, and your convictions are gifts from the Spirit of God, so be thankful! Thank God that His care extends to the finest of details. He accepts your worship in what you cannot do and mine in what I can do. Gratitude, gratitude, gratitude is to rule our attitude.

x   Recognize that you are not an island nor do you sit on a throne (v. 7). Paul Simon got this one wrong. We are not rocks or islands—we are not that strong. We cannot resist the winds or waves of self-interest apart from the might of Christ Himself. We are able only as we cling to our Gibraltar, our unmovable Jesus. No one will be judged by our standard; our interpretation of the Scriptures will not be the final arbiter of any man's fate. Truth emits from and will be interpreted by God and God only. We see through a glass darkly.

x   Recognize your ownership—you are Christ's slave (vv. 8–9). Slave is not a popular word, but that is the word used here. In fact, most Bible versions have neutered the passages in which it appears and have substituted "servant" to take the edge off. The word is slave, and our Master is austere. These rules of conduct we have been speaking of are mandates from our Master. Slaves don't disobey without grave consequences. If we are "Can'ts", then we must do what God orders "Can'ts" to do. The consequences of disobedience can be earth-shaking.

x Ask yourself why you are pronouncing judgment (vv. 10–12). The question is, "Why do you judge your brother?" What's your answer? God's response is to take care of yourself: you'll be responsible to Him for yourself—not for your brother. Don't you have your hands full with your own battles against sin? Can you fight your brother's battles and win yours at the same time? When we turn from our own battle to fight someone else's, we give the enemy a broadside shot at our vulnerable backside. He will not often miss with that kind of opening.

x Remember that you will stand before the judgment seat as well (vv. 10–12). We've probably already said enough here. (See Rev. 14:7 and Eccl. 12:13–14.)

x Stop passing judgment! (v. 13). Is that clear enough? Stop it! You and I don't have the stature or the right. Cease being a doctrinal Nazi! Our role is to serve our brothers and sisters; God's role is to judge them.

OUR ROLE IS TO SERVE OUR BROTHERS AND SISTERS; IT IS GOD'S ROLE TO JUDGE THEM.

x Recognize that others have liberty in Christ (v. 14). This is an extremely difficult threshold for a "Can't"; will you enter here with me? If we stand at the door, peek in, and watch our brothers and sisters doing that which we are forbidden to do, we shrink back. A tide of emotion rises within us that is nearly uncontrollable. It's like turning on a computer: it boots up to its default settings every time. In this case, the default feels like righteous indignation. It may be, but in this instance it is misplaced. That tide of emotion rose because our minds went immediately to judgment—our default setting. Our sensibilities were offended, but we made an unfair conclusion. We judged that person as being wrong, unholy, loose, or sinful. Examine your response closely. I think you'll find this close to the mark. Rather than judging another from a place of offense, our calling is to grant liberty to others and to keep our own conscience clean. We are not to condemn the conscience of another. This may be the single most difficult thing for a "Can't" to accomplish. Our system set-up is defaulted to judgment; recognize that these Scriptures are the reset instructions for that default setting. Change your settings to these twenty responses, and your system will be in tune with the Holy Spirit of God.

x   Recognize that you may not have that same liberty that others do (v. 14). Relax! Live within the circle of your own conscience. Don't let the liberty of others make you miserable. Your anger and discomfort doesn't affect them for an instant. (Unless of course you unleashed it upon them in defiance of the apostle's instructions.) Be content in the embrace of God as you are; no one can take that from you.

RATHER THAN JUDGING ANOTHER FROM A PLACE OF OFFENSE, OUR CALLING IS TO GRANT LIBERTY TO OTHERS AND TO KEEP OUR OWN CONSCIENCE CLEAN.

x   Recognize that the kingdom of God does not revolve around do's and don'ts (v. 17). Its heart is righteousness (through Christ, not works), peace, and joy. Let's address something that may be happening about now. Is it possible that your insistence on your convictions, or your offense at another's liberty, is eating at you? Could this be because your convictions are not truly yours? I challenged you on this before: did you wrestle with the questions and win them by hard study and diligent prayer before the throne? Are you trying to uphold issues simply because of the company you keep or the teachers you hear? Are you attempting to conform to a list of extrabiblical do's and don'ts? Do you want to overcome the empty severity of that? Then meditate on what Paul means by righteousness, peace, and joy. If you will make a diligent study of these three attributes, you will find a world of relief. Once we discover what God has in store for us here, we will escape the inner turmoil of a judgmental outlook.

x Realize that you are acceptable to God and approved by men when you serve others in this way (v. 18). To be accepted in the beloved is our undisputed position in Christ (see Eph. 1:1–14). Living this out practically is our calling. Ephesians is a great book to study on this. The first three chapters are a statement of our position in Christ, the last three chapters are the practical outworking of that standing. Get intimately attuned to this letter and you will fulfill this instruction.

x Pursue peace and mutual edification (v. 19). Pursue is not a lethargic word. It is the word choice of active energy. Football coaches love this word; ask any defensive backs coach what he wants his secondary to do. Ask Mike Singletary or Ray Lewis (both great middle linebackers in the NFL) what a great defensive player does. They pursue the ball—wherever it is. Whatever or whomever is between them and the ball, beware! These men hunt like starving men. Does your fellowship stalk peace? Does it chase down harmony, hunt it, and seize it? Do you personally seek it? Will you wrestle for it, fight for it, and discipline yourself for it? Remember that it was second-most on the mind of Christ the night before He died—it's worth the pursuit!

x   Keep your conscience clear before God (v.22). This is a great follow up to #1—if you can't, don't. It is not worth it to defile your conscience. God calls that sin. Paul's reminder was that if you think it's sin, it is—for you.

x   Be joyful in your convictions (v.22). The battle may be rough here, because our convictions are constantly under assault. Stick to your guns joyfully, without a sour attitude. 1 John 3:21–22 encourages us that if our heart does not condemn us, we have confidence before God and our prayers will be answered because we keep His commandments and do that which is pleasing to Him. Do not minimize the preciousness of your convictions. Do not condemn yourself—don't beat yourself up over them. Also, do not sacrifice them for any reason other than the direct call of God to lay them aside. They are part and parcel of your spiritual walk; in a sense they "approve" you before God because they are a measure of your grace-enabled obedience.

x   Don't do it if you doubt (v.23). Don't condemn yourself to a guilty conscience. Proceed with the faith you have; live within the circle of your faith (conscience). This summarizes everything above—faith frees us not to eat. Faith frees us to walk in our convictions without condemning our conscience. Doubt destroys this delicate balance. Whatever you do—don't offend your conscience. If your brother who has liberty pushes you (in opposition to his instructions), resist him and politely insist in Jesus's name that he back off. Resist the urge to judge him for his freedom. Resist the urge to try to convince him. Drop the subject unless you and he are strong enough to debate the issue without losing love or unity.

What do you think? Those are the weak-in-faith-man's twenty. Twenty bullet points for living in harmony with brothers who do things we cannot in conscience do. While the strong man's twenty are different, they are no less difficult to maintain. The strong believer must learn to show deference in humility, while the weak believer must learn to show tolerance in humility. Those of us who can't must tolerate those who can. Biblical tolerance is much different than that defined in the world today. It is not an "anything goes" indifference for the sake of peace. It is an active gift of grace toward those whose behavior and attitudes have the potential to hurt us. Those who can't, give to those who can, a gift wrapped in the love of Christ. We willingly offer grace and suppress judgment. This is pleasing in God's sight. Wearing this attitude will prepare us for the inevitable difficulties that come when sinful people join together under the grace of Christ. Acting out these qualities will arrest the progress of the autoimmune disease the Church is suffering.

CHRISTIAN TOLERANCE IS AN ACTIVE GIFT OF GRACE TOWARD THOSE WHOSE BEHAVIOR AND ATTITUDES HAVE THE POTENTIAL TO HURT US. THE STRONG BELIEVER MUST LEARN TO SHOW DEFERENCE IN HUMILITY, WHILE THE WEAK BELIEVER MUST LEARN TO SHOW TOLERANCE IN HUMILITY.

HANDLING CONFLICT BETWEEN "CANS" AND "CAN'TS"

Conflict comes with closeness. When believers are called to work together, they bring their personal history with them. They bring their convictions and their preferences and their personalities. "Cans" in close proximity with "Can'ts" are bound to rub one another the wrong way from time to time. What do we do when conflict knocks on our door? How do we address offenses in the Body? Let me address the "Can'ts" first.

Are you convinced of the necessity of having the conversation? Is the liberty expressed by your "Can" brother compromising your conscience? If so, by all means let him know, but do it in love—not judgment and anger! He knows what he is to do—he will limit his liberty for the sake of your conscience. What if that's not enough? What if you really feel the need to convince him of your point of view? I don't see a prohibition for you to attempt to convince him, but I see a great danger. If you are edgy and offended, the conversation may degenerate into an argument. That won't accomplish anything. If you are sincere, not easily agitated, and willing to walk away from the conversation in love regardless of the outcome—then go for it!

To my "Can" brother. If you detect that your brother is approaching you in sincerity with no agitation or irritation, then engage the conversation gently. Allow him to express himself fully. Listen carefully. Follow the strong man's twenty. Show deference and love. Be willing to limit your liberty. Then, if he asks your point of view, explain very simply from the Scriptures what you are confident of without trying to convince him. The Spirit will work His own will. There is no need for you to press the point home. It's a tough conversation for a "Can't", so please don't add any difficulty to it.

I understand the difficulty a "Can't" has with this chapter. I feel the tension these instructions cause. Remember that I confessed that I'm a doctrinal Nazi. I care about the truth. I want to weasel out of these twenty points. I want to misapply them. I want to label these as "so-called" liberties so I can dismiss them neatly. I want to deny that they have anything to do with my issues. I don't like considering myself as weak. I think there are things that are simply wrong for any Christian to practice, even if I can't give a black and white Bible passage. I think some Christians play fast and loose with the text of Scripture, and I have trouble with their novel interpretations. These things bother me! I could go on with a number of reasons why I'm not fond of God's approach here, but none of them excuse me. I must obey, and let God sort it out.

You may be feeling the same tension, but my hope is that you will not fall to the temptation to dismiss the truth here. Will you meditate on it? Will you study it and let it penetrate your mind? Will you write down your objections and questions and discuss them with your Father? Will you strive for the unity and harmony of the Body? If we meet some day, can we have a loving and joyful discussion over our differences? I'm looking forward to binding as many brothers as I can to myself in peace. I want a taste of that harmony we will enjoy in the presence of God. I want a glimpse of what it will be like when all of our questions are answered and all of our differences are erased. I hope you share the same desire.

I'm not a Pollyanna about this though. I realize that there are some natural and tough questions that arise out of this discussion. What about doctrine—where do we draw the line? Aren't there some issues that just can't be dealt with this way? What is essential and what is negotiable in the Christian faith? When do I separate from a disobedient brother? Are there any examples in the Scripture that will help us decide when the line has been crossed? I don't think we could do justice to the topic of unity if we don't also explore the topic of Biblical separation. We'll do that in the next two chapters.

GOD IS A FATHER, AND HE FATHERS EVERY ONE OF HIS CHILDREN ACCORDING TO THEIR INDIVIDUAL NEEDS AND THEIR LEVEL OF MATURITY.

CHAPTER EIGHT

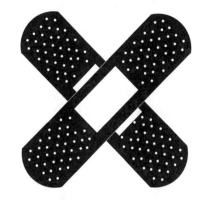

MY DOCTRINE'S PURE. WHAT ABOUT YOURS?

IN 1896, A BATTLE BROKE out. Invectives flew. Both sides joined the fracas, entrenched as enemies. Churches, districts, state organizations, and an entire national denomination got tied up in it. Reconciliation was attempted but thwarted when one personality or the other rose up to contest the validity or the outcome of the process. For three years the battle raged on. It was characterized by stubbornness, misunderstanding, character assassination, and unreasonable demands. A prominent, seemingly gentle, reasonable, and gracious man had his reputation ruined and was driven from his profession. Others were deeply hurt, disillusioned, and harshly treated by the whole atmosphere of argument.

The fascinating thing about this battle is the cause. It would be almost laughable if it had not had such serious consequences. A seminary historian (and professor and president) had discovered an inconsistency in some facts that many had previously understood to be indisputable. W.H. Whitsitt, then president of the Southern Baptist Theological Seminary, had travelled to England to do some research. He discovered, to his surprise, that the English Baptists had not practiced baptism by immersion until around 1641. Before that, they had baptized by sprinkling or pouring. That's an interesting fact that really doesn't challenge any biblical convictions. It simply means that one era of Baptist practitioners used a different mode of baptism. Curiously, Whitsitt made no case for changing any practice in the Southern Baptist Convention. He merely stated the facts. He wasn't looking for controversy.

THOSE OF US WHO LOVE TRUTH AND HAVE NO RESERVATIONS FIGHTING FOR IT ARE OFTEN BLIND TO THE FALLOUT OF OUR ACTIONS.

Whitsitt published his remarks on the discovery. You wouldn't think it, but his remarks ignited a firestorm. He was accused of undermining the "truth" that Christians had practiced baptism by immersion since John the Baptist, and that true Baptists had never done anything differently. He was excoriated in numerous denominational publications. His resignation or dismissal from the seminary was demanded. Hours were spent in debate, motions were made, resolutions written, and all were hotly championed.

All this commotion raged despite the fact that Whitsitt made no attempt whatsoever to change anyone's mind on the acceptable mode of baptism. He remained a staunch advocate that the only truly Biblical mode of baptism was immersion. Do you find this incredible? Are Christian men and women really threatened by a factual timeline change that doesn't materially change the doctrine? Do you suppose Jesus gets fired up over such things? The outcome of this incident was tragic and instructive. Mr. Whitsitt lost his job, many of his opponents lost face, and years later apologies had to be made. But the damage was already done.

The tragic reality is that a very small match can detonate an immense explosion. Those of us who love truth and have no reservations fighting for it are often blind to the fallout of our actions. Speaking for myself and I'm sure many others, we too often fire a cannon where a peashooter would do.

What do we do with this tension between pure doctrine and brotherly love?

Paul's instructions in Romans and 1 Corinthians seem to say, "put away the cannon." I can almost hear God say, "Truth is Mine; I'll guard it. It won't fall down under the weight of a few weaker (or stronger) brothers." There is a way to stay true to our convictions yet still love our brothers and sisters. Of course I'm limiting my discussion to professing Christians and non-essential Christian doctrine. I'm not referring to the defense of essential truth, where demonically energized enemies are attempting to destroy it. In that case, we are called to "earnestly contend for the faith" (Jude 3).

In the case of our Christian brother, the approach is different. The question is, "Do we believe that God will work out the truth in the heart of someone who is a true believer? Is He capable? Can He be thwarted in that occupation?" Jude 24–25 says, "Now to Him who is able to keep you from stumbling, and to make you stand in the presence of His glory blameless with great joy, to the only God our Savior, through Jesus Christ our Lord, be glory, majesty, dominion, and authority, before all time and now and forever. Amen." I think "blameless" would have to include our stand in the truth. I think we can be kept from stumbling in our under-standing of the truth. I believe what God says here. He is able to make us blameless in these matters. The assurance we have in dealing with brothers is that one day they will stand blameless before God. God takes the responsibility upon Himself to work that out in partnership with every believer. We can trust Him on that score.

So the question then turns to essentials. What doctrines must be held in order for us to consider ourselves truly Christian? I'm probably opening a huge can of worms here. We may not agree on the essentials—you may want to add or take away one or two. My hope is that even if you don't see all of these doctrines as essen-tial, we will at least agree that they are extremely important. To lose the critical meaning of any one of these doctrines would be to seriously undermine the Word of God and the Christian faith. If you feel the need to add to the list, I hope you will carefully review the historic, orthodox position on the doctrine. Has the historic, orthodox Church seen your inclusion as a necessary or essential doctrine in its writings or creeds? If you subtract from the list, I hope you'll reflect on the potential consequences of re-moving the doctrine from the list.

Since I don't have the time or the scholarly credentials to re-search and carefully document a historical list, I had to rely on others. It's not an easy task, though. Distilling centuries of saintly work, slogging through books, blogs, and binders, and separat-ing human agendas from actual Bible directives is touchy work. Some believers are content with the Apostles' Creed, some with the Nicene, and others with yet more creeds laid down by godly scholars through the ages of the Church. I'm not convinced there has ever been a strict consensus on every point of essential doc-trine. That doesn't mean we can't come very close.

Presenting a list like this is also inherently dangerous since we don't have the ability in this book to explain our choices or expound upon the doctrines. Suffice it to say that there is no attempt to exclude any person's point of view on the matter. We are simply trying to get to the consensus of orthodox, conservative, and godly scholarship on essential doctrine.

The list below was compiled by me from an article published by the Christian Research Journal and written by Norman L. Geisler, Distinguished Professor of Apologetics at Veritas Evangelical Seminary. I like brother Geisler's approach, so I've chosen to use it. I could have used any of the approximately twenty-five lists I found in books, online apologetic sites, etc. I chose this one because brother Geisler may be the most well-known modern apologist for our faith, and the article contains some very good reasoning for his choices that I think we can all benefit by. The entire article is reprinted by permission in the Appendix. I hope you'll take the time to carefully read it. Without further adieu: The List.

THE LIST OF ESSENTIALS

The list of essential Christian doctrines that emerge from the early creeds and councils includes:

x   Human depravity,
x   Christ's virgin birth,
x   Christ's sinlessness,
x   Christ's deity,
x   Christ's humanity,
x   God's unity,
x   God's triunity,
x   The necessity of God's grace,
x   The necessity of faith,
x   Christ's atoning death,

x   Christ's bodily resurrection,
x   Christ's bodily ascension,
x   Christ's present high priestly service, and
x   Christ's second coming, final judgment (heaven and hell), and reign.

All of these are necessary for salvation to be possible in the broad sense, which includes justification, sanctification, and glorification.

It is not necessary, however, to believe all of these to be saved (justified). The minimum necessary to believe in order to be saved is: (1) human depravity, (3) Christ's sinlessness, (4) Christ's deity, (5) Christ's humanity, (6) God's unity, (7) God's triunity, (8) the necessity of God's grace, (9) the necessity of faith, (10) Christ's atoning death, and (11) Christ's bodily resurrection.

It is not necessary to believe in (2) Christ's virgin birth, (12) Christ's bodily ascension, (13) Christ's present service, or (14) Christ's second coming and final judgment as a condition for obtaining a right standing with God (justification). Even some of those beliefs that are necessary may be more implicit than explicit; for example, human depravity and God's triunity. Regarding human depravity, one must believe that he is a sinner in need of a Savior, but need not believe all that the orthodox doctrine of human depravity involves, such as the inheritance of a sin nature. The deity of Christ, likewise, is involved, which in turn involves at least two persons who are God (the Father and the Son); but there is no reason to think that to be saved one must understand and explicitly believe the orthodox doctrine of the personality and deity of the Holy Spirit who is united with those two persons in one nature (i.e., one God). Many people, in fact, do not understand this doctrine clearly, even years after they were saved.

All of the essential doctrines are necessary to make salvation possible, but not all are essential for one to believe in order for one to be saved. All are essential to believe to be a consistent Christian, but not all are necessary to believe to become a Christian. Generally, a sign that authentic conversion has occurred is that when a professing believer is instructed on these doctrines, he embraces them."[5]

These are the concluding paragraphs to the full article. They are enough to give us the raw list of essential Christian doctrine as regards our salvation. I think Geisler is right in limiting essential Christian doctrine to the list above. Christ rightly remains the center of Christian doctrine for Geisler and, I believe, for us. It may also be true that once we move beyond these essentials is when the trouble starts. I wouldn't suggest that we completely neglect issues outside these essentials, but rather that we exercise extreme caution and grace in our discussions of them.

We can safely describe any doctrine outside these named by Geisler as non-essential. We can also include that many of the finer points of these doctrines are non-essential. Note that we are not saying that doctrines not on Geisler's list are unimportant or expendable—nothing of the sort! We are simply saying that these listed doctrines are the ones that define Christianity. Without them, Christianity becomes something else. Without many others we might name that Christians disagree on, Christianity remains the same.

---

5   Norman L. Geisler, "The Essential Doctrines of the Christian Faith," Christian Research Journal 28, no. 6 (2005): http://www.equip.org/articles/the-essential-doctrines-of-the-christian-faith-part-one/.

We could certainly find plenty to battle over as in the Whitsitt Controversy, but can't we rather find much to agree upon? If we are in agreement over the basic statements, then we should be able to embrace one another as brothers. Let's vigorously debate the finer points. If we disagree within the bounds of essential doctrine, then we can embrace and walk away as loving brothers. On the other hand, we cannot write flaming pamphlets and blogs aimed at character assassination and expect God to bless our "stand for the truth." As the apostle James says, we cannot "bless our Lord and Father, and . . . curse men."

Consider also these words of James, chapter 4.

> What is the source of quarrels and conflicts among you? Is not the source your pleasures that wage war in your members? You lust and do not have; so you commit murder. You are envious and cannot obtain; so you fight and quarrel. You do not have because you do not ask. You ask and do not receive, because you ask with wrong motives, so that you may spend it on your pleasures.

Also,

> Humble yourselves in the presence of the Lord, and He will exalt you. Do not speak against one another, brethren. He who speaks against a brother or judges his brother, speaks against the law and judges the law; but if you judge the law, you are not a doer of the law but a judge of it. There is only one Lawgiver and Judge, the One who is able to save and to destroy; but who are you who judge your neighbor?

Maybe we can speak kindly to our brothers with whom we disagree. Maybe we can simply, humbly ask God for a change in our brother's heart. Maybe He'll graciously change our heart in the process. Maybe we'll find a way to kill our pride and love our brother. Maybe we'll discipline ourselves to disagree while exhibiting affectionate kindness. Maybe we'll defer to the weaker brother. Maybe we'll honor Christ and exalt His Gospel. Maybe we'll see the world stop and pay attention to this new Love. Maybe . . .

Maybe we can be obstinate in our obedience. How are you seeing things now, my brother? Has the Spirit said anything that sticks on this topic? Have the Scriptures detained you? Have you wrestled with your role in the Body? What decisions have you come to? Are you committing yourself to this newly discovered truth?

WE SHOULD DISCIPLINE OURSELVES TO EXHIBIT AFFECTIONATE KINDNESS WHEN DISAGREEING.

It doesn't matter what your standing is. You may be a professor charged with teaching the next generation of scholars. You may be a pastor tending to Christ's sheep. You may be leader of a movement, one to whom many resort for wisdom and perspective. You may be a new Christian, unfamiliar with the ground we've covered. You may be a stalwart and long-standing member of your church. You may be a disconnected, hurt disciple. Wherever you find yourself, you must find yourself obedient. The stakes are too high for us to fail here.

CHAPTER NINE

WHERE DO WE DRAW THE LINE?

I BELIEVE THAT EVERYTHING WE'VE shared up till now begs a question. The question is, "At what point do we separate from a brother?" In other words, "Do the Scriptures give us a hard guideline for deciding what constitutes an offense so grievous that we have to part ways?"

If our primary concern is to maintain the unity of the Body without abandoning truth, then there must be some direction for dealing with sin and unrepentance when they are found in the Church. As we have seen, it is a sin to create division over matters of conscience or doctrinal distinctives. But what about immorality, or false teaching where essentials are concerned, or other sins, especially when we find no repentance? What do we do in these cases?

I'm happy to say that the Bible is not silent here. We have several illustrations in New Testament life that shed light on this question. Interestingly, they are few and far between: much fewer than some would have us believe. The occurrences and circumstances surrounding them are so rare and painful that we could miss them if we were not tuned to them. They are extreme occasions. They are full of rebellion, falsehood, pride, and antagonism. Fortunately, they are swiftly and decisively dealt with. The apostles had no patience for anything that would actually blemish the Bride.

Let's clarify the people we are talking about. We are not including unbelievers who make no profession of Christ, are not a part of any local church, and who make no claims of fellowship in the Gospel. Paul says in 1 Corinthians 5 that if we were to avoid these folks, we would have to leave the earth. That's not a very practical way to live out our Christian lives. We are including unbelievers who profess to know Christ, are part of a local church, and make claims of having fellowship in the Gospel. We are also including believers who fit these descriptions. Jesus includes both of these in the kingdom by giving us the parable of the wheat and the tares. Both will grow up together in the Church and will only be separated in the judgment. He made it very clear that we will not always be able to discern the difference.

DO THE SCRIPTURES GIVE US A HARD GUIDELINE FOR DECIDING WHEN WE SHOULD PART WAYS WITH A BROTHER OR SISTER?

How did the Apostles deal with these folks and the events that revealed their deeds? First Corinthians 5 is perhaps the most instructive passage along these lines. The case is of peculiar interest. A man, by deduction a member of the Church, was committing adultery with his stepmother; something Paul said didn't even happen among the pagans. The church was happily allowing him to continue his sin while letting him enjoy all the benefits of church fellowship. This is also a pure case against that attitude that would sacrifice truth and replace it with pseudo-love or, in modern parlance, enabling behavior.

Paul only needed to hear about this situation remotely. He was swift in his condemnation of the practice and the Corinthian's acceptance of it. By accepting the man, they were, in effect, accepting the sin. Paul's decision was clear: "In the name of our Lord Jesus, when you are assembled, and I with you in spirit, with the power of our Lord Jesus . . . deliver such a one to Satan for the destruction of his flesh, so that his spirit may be saved in the day of the Lord Jesus." We may not understand all that is meant by "delivering someone over to Satan for the destruction of the flesh," but whatever it means it can't be pleasant. This is a painful punishment. This is a bomb dropped into an unsuspecting, enabling congregation. What a hard word to hear! Doesn't this militate against love? No, my brother, this is love. Paul made sure to exercise this tough love in the name and power of our Lord Jesus.

Paul goes on to clarify part of what he means by turning someone over to Satan. In verse 11 he tells the Corinthians not to associate with any so-called brother if he is an immoral person. That's pretty clear. It means don't hang around with him. Don't keep company with him. The Anabaptists called it "shunning." We are to purposefully avoid any brother or so-called brother who is openly immoral and unrepentant. We have to assume that he was unrepentant, because Paul writes with the full expectation that this action will end in the man's spirit being saved "in the day of the Lord Jesus." Paul's expectation was that this action would lead the man to repent. It's painful, but it's worthwhile! What a joy when one so treated repents!

There are further details we often miss in this passage. Paul continues the thought about not associating with brothers or sisters practicing immorality by including those who are "covetous, or an idolater, or a reviler, or a drunkard, or a swindler—not even to eat with such a one." When did you last hear of a church actually taking action on these instructions? Did you ever see a church disfellowship an unrepentant (don't miss the emphasis) covetous person, or alcoholic, or swindler, or heaven forbid—someone who reviled (uses abusive or contemptuous speech) a brother in Christ? This is such a rarity these days! Could this be part of the reason we have so many dysfunctional churches?

THERE IS NOTHING MORE PROFOUNDLY BEAUTIFUL THAN SEEING SOMEONE COME BACK TO CHRIST AND BROTHERLY FELLOWSHIP.

I was very privileged for many years to be a part of a church that took the practice of church discipline seriously. I witnessed several occasions (one involving a very close friend) of members undergoing church discipline. Being involved in these circumstances was akin to being in the waiting room while a dear one is in surgery. It is tense to await the outcome of such drastic measures. When surgery is necessary for the diseases of the soul, the wait for God to do His work can be tough. To me, it is always painful and heartbreaking. Fortunately, I never saw it done in anger or pride by the leadership. Outcomes were varied. Some church members submitted to the discipline and repented publicly. Those were sweet times—there is nothing more profound and deeply beautiful than seeing someone come back to Christ and brotherly fellowship! On the other hand, some resisted, left the Church, and plunged into whatever they were headed toward. I know that twenty-some years later some of them are still living apart from Christ. Devastating!

As a pastor, I have only been involved in two instances of church discipline. One subject experienced a beautiful restoration through repentance, the other an angry separation due to hardness and unwillingness to repent. Both were extremely difficult times for me personally and for our congregation. What we found is that God remains faithful if we will just do things His way. We are not able to see all the ramifications of either of these instances, but we are rejoicing in a restored brother and praying for the one we lost. Our confidence is that the Lord will perfect our imperfect obedience.

The overarching point is that there are situations that demand we separate from a brother. We don't even eat with him! The clear teaching here is that when we find gross immorality, divisive behavior, and unrepentance, it clearly qualifies a brother for strict disciplinary measures. There are other situations that demand the same.

Romans 16:17 clearly delineates another such offense that calls us to separation. "Now I urge you, brethren, keep your eye on those who cause dissensions and hindrances contrary to the teaching which you learned, and turn away from them." Say, isn't this what we've been talking about all this time? Paul is telling us to divide from those who cause division. That's most ironic. The qualifier is "contrary to the teaching." Paul is really addressing false teaching here. He's instructing us to separate from those who bring false teaching that divides the Church. Novel ideas that run contrary to apostolic teaching are not welcome. We could sum it up as "divisive heresy." Titus 3:10, 2 Peter 2, 2 John 10–11, and 3 John 9–10 all describe such people and their teachings.

Put a stake in the ground here. Teaching contrary to apostolic teaching is not tolerated by God! In Galatians 1:8, Paul calls all who would bring contrary teaching into the Church accursed—no matter if they are angels or men. That's hard, un-compromising language. Listen to how he instructs Timothy:

> If anyone advocates a different doctrine and does not agree with sound words, those of our Lord Jesus Christ, and with the doctrine conforming to godliness, he is conceited and understands nothing; but he has a morbid interest in controversial questions and disputes about words, out of which arise envy, strife, abusive language, evil suspicions, and constant friction between men of depraved mind and deprived of the truth, who suppose that godliness is a means of gain. – 1 Timothy 6:3–5

Again, tough words! They are words of a spiritual father protecting his children. No honorable father would look the other way while lying, unprincipled men molested their children. Paul is no different, as he walks in the character of our heavenly Father. He calls out false teachers in order to keep peace, truth, and love among true believers. We must recognize that this is unifying language from Paul. Believers, especially spiritual leaders, should have a holy passion to present a unified front against false teaching. The loving defense of truth maintains unity.

THE LOVING DEFENSE OF TRUTH MAINTAINS UNITY.

Other clear instances of demanded separation are blasphemy (1 Tim. 1:20), those who lead undisciplined lives contrary to Paul's teaching (2 Thess. 3:6), and disobedience to the clear instruction of God's Word (2 Thess. 3:14). Note that Paul says not to associate with them, but at the same time we are not to regard them as enemies, but admonish them as brothers. What an important distinction! Again, we are assuming that these are cases that also include an unrepentant attitude. If someone repents we must defer to Jesus's

teaching in Matthew 18 and consider them a brother won! I think
James paints a portrait of God's gentle heart in these matters.

> My brethren, if any among you strays from the truth and
> one turns him back, let him know that he who turns a
> sinner from the error of his way will save his soul from
> death and will cover a multitude of sins. – James 5:19–20

What a sweet promise. Don't you want to save some souls
from death and cover multitudes of sins? Let's not delight in un-
covering sin! Too many of us find it satisfying to uncover another's imperfections and temptations. This is a ghastly trait—fight
hard against it when you sense it rising! If we will put on humility and approach our brothers in love, "taking heed to ourselves
lest we also fall," then we will certainly win many back to the
arms of Christ.

TO SEPARATE FROM THE WORLD IS COMMANDED, TO SEPARATE FROM A BROTHER IS (ALMOST ALWAYS) CONDEMNED.

This is a short chapter and intentionally so. Dividing from
Christian brothers and sisters is de-emphasized in Scripture.
I have some dear brothers who loudly contend that they are
"Separatists." Some of them are truly encouraging their people to
stay separate from the world and its encroaching influence: amen
to them! Some are bellowing in pride that their holiness is somehow more holy than my holiness—shame on them! I don't see any
encouragement from Christ or the apostles to make separatism
(from fellow Christians) a banner to rally under or a hill to die on.

To define the difference in approach, we could say that to separate from the world is commanded, to separate from a brother is
condemned (in all but a few extreme cases).

The end goal, even in separation, is reconciliation and unity.
It is healing and avoidance of further damage from disease.

Separation is a stepping-stone to unity and is to be used only in extreme cases. It's treated much like Moses treated divorce—he permitted it because of the "hardness of their hearts." I think the Lord permits separation only because He knows that some people have hard, unrepentant hearts. We should look at it as the last resort, and for the purpose of reconciliation, never anticipating it to be a permanent arrangement. Divorce is painful, the tearing of flesh, so also is separation for the sake of discipline and reconciliation. We should enter this territory in sackcloth and ashes, head downcast, heart open wide for our brother, and fully transparent before our God lest our own sin find us out.

CHAPTER TEN

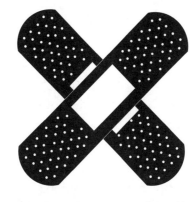

THE DELIGHT
OF CHRIST

DO YOU STILL SENSE THAT we don't yet have a firm grasp on the precise approach to all these questions? If so, I'm with you. After studying for years, meditating specifically for several of those years, and writing on the topic for months, I still find myself a bit liquid. I think if you turn me one way all my substance will flow that way, turn me the other and I'll flow that way. Balance is elusive. My equilibrium is upset if I push any of these propositions too hard.

GOD'S GRACE IS WILD AND UNTAMED; IT REFUSES TO BE QUANTIFIED OR EVALUATED INSIDE MY LITTLE GOD-BOX.

I want for something solid, unwavering—a black and white commandment—to rule all. I realize that trouble is wound up in that desire. That desire binds me to Law. It imprisons me to legalism. Grace invites me to run free with the wind of the Spirit. Go where He goes—act within His borders of love, forgiveness, kindness, gentleness. Do the impossible, embrace the adventure—be like Christ. That's hard. Rules are cozy couches I can sink into. I can measure myself against rules. Grace is wild and can't be quantified or evaluated inside my little God-box. These circumstances we have been considering often wiggle out of our cage of rules. They get slippery and difficult to handle. We can't lower the gavel and make granite pronouncements, so we often shrink back from the challenge.

How much easier it is to write about these things than to live them! My mind cries out for my Savior! I need Jesus. I need supernatural power and spiritual muscle beyond my means. I'm incredibly excited about these things while sitting here in my study. In fact, I'm pretty good at working through all these scenarios in my mind in the safety of my office chair. But what will happen once I step outside my little comfy space? I'm fairly certain that everything I've written will be profoundly challenged and I'll find myself desperately clinging to the threads of character I described in Chapter 5. What will I do then? I hope to turn to this last chapter and remind myself of what I'm about to remind you. None of what we have described can or will happen without a decisive and complete abandonment of everything we call our own, including our liberties and our non-essential convictions. We must reject and desert every vestige of self-sufficiency in favor of a full and absolute freefall into the heart of Christ. I think Colossians 2 pictures this for us.

WE MUST REJECT EVERY VESTIGE OF SELF-SUFFICIENCY IN FAVOR
OF A FULL AND ABSOLUTE FREEFALL INTO THE HEART OF CHRIST.

You'll find there in verses 13–15 a grim picture of our condition.
We are dead in trespasses, unable to communicate with God (uncircumcised), drowning in insurmountable debt to the Law, and
legally bound to pay that impossible debt. Unlike so many stories
that find the victim suffering unjustly, we deserve this disaster;
we consciously decided to wallow in this misery. When we knew
God, we did not glorify Him as God (see Romans 1). We rejected
Him. All of us reside here in our old man. We need a benefactor
strong enough to overcome our chains.

Into that prison rides a Warrior Captain bent on rescuing us
from this ruin of our own making. He pours onto the scene like
molten fire, eyes ablaze, every muscle and sinew taut and agitated.
Sword unsheathed and awake, free hand with an iron grip on
the reigns of grace. In His train are the myriads upon myriads of
heavens' freed men—companions in our toil, fully aware of our
predicament. He rides down upon our captivity and unleashes
Almighty wrath upon our most ferocious enemies. Look how He
conquers! Look who He conquers!

A great sweep of His sword—Death dies! Life springs
forth! (v. 13).

Another blow—Debt expires! Freedom is kindled in the
wind! (v. 14).

He dismounts, snatches the decrees written against us, and
with hammer-rings of triumph He nails them to His cross with
the butt of His sword. Done! (v. 14).

Hand-to hand-battle now ensues against pitched opposition.
Savage slave masters, bent on keeping their prizes, wage brutal
war. With an immense curving stroke He dispatches them, dis-
arms them, and displays their defeat to all. He marches the van-
quished rulers and authorities in all their unholy array before

the astonished crowds; they are now fully exposed and submitted to overwhelming Authority. He stands invincible, glittering in unassailable Glory! My Champion, your Champion, Liberator of every law-enslaved, devil-accused, broken-spirited, spiritually mutilated soul (v. 15).

He then turns and invites us to leave our prison and join the procession. Not at the end, but as it were, in company with Him! Then He says to us,

"Therefore . . ." (v. 16):

No one has the standing to judge you for what you eat or drink.

No one has the authority to judge you for the days you observe.

Serve not shadows—Christ is the substance! (v. 16–17).

Let no one tempt you to false humility or false worship.

Let no one tease you with his visions or inflated claims.

Follow no phantoms—Christ is the head! (v. 18–19).

Die to the world.

Die to empty decrees, "Do not handle, do not taste, do not touch!"

Die to appearances.

Die to self-made religion, self-abasement, and severe self-abuse.

Die with Christ and live! (vv. 20–23; ch. 3:3).

Seek the things above: Christ is there, on the right hand of God!

Set your affection on the things above: Christ is there, and your life is in Him!

Wait patiently for your redemption.

Christ is redemption, your Life, your Glory, your God! (ch. 3:3–4).

This is what I need! A constant, all-consuming focus on Christ! I need Christ to be BIG! I need His gentle, wounded hands to cradle my face and keep me tuned to His brilliance. I need the inviting assurance of His voice pleading, "Look at Me. Look at Me. Look at Me." I need to be lifted out of the blast of war and carried tightly to His heart, suspended above my fears and enemies, helpless upon His mercy. I need relief from the wrack and crash of conflict. I need rest and an absence of noise. I need companions who will walk with me following my Helper. I need Jesus and I need His brothers and sisters. I need wellness in His Body. I need Love.

I NEED A CONSTANT, ALL-CONSUMING FOCUS ON CHRIST!

If your heart cries like mine, brother or sister, then why don't you join me? Why don't we walk together down this long and difficult path of unity? Is there a chance we might get past our short-sighted humanity to see the full light of God's glorious day? Can we be brothers and sisters "called in one hope" (Eph.4:4) rather than "so-called" Christians? Might we discover true brotherhood, locked-arm companionship, full-faced honor, and unmerited, indefinable Love? Can we be healers of the autoimmune destruction left by the disease of divisiveness? Do you think that's possible in Christ? I do! It's His undying passion. It's His always-afire zeal. It's His open-hearted appeal to the Father. It's His determined delight! Why wouldn't He throw down every barrier and banish every enemy that resists this?

Unity proves Presence. Unity expresses Righteousness, Peace, and Joy. Unity reflects God. Unity proves Love. Love never fails.

CONCLUSION

HOW MUCH DO WE LOVE?

If I were to speak with the combined eloquence of men and angels I should stir men like a fanfare of trumpets or the crashing of cymbals, but unless I had love, I should do nothing more. If I had the gift of foretelling the future and had in my mind not only all human knowledge but the secrets of God, and if, in addition, I had that absolute faith which can move mountains, but had no love, I tell you I should amount to nothing at all. If I were to sell all my possessions to feed the hungry and, for my convictions, allowed my body to be burned, and yet had no love, I should achieve precisely nothing.

This love of which I speak is slow to lose patience—it looks for a way of being constructive. It is not possessive: it is neither anxious to impress nor does it cherish inflated ideas of its own importance.

Love has good manners and does not pursue selfish advantage. It is not touchy. It does not keep account of evil or gloat over the wickedness of other people. On the contrary, it is glad with all good men when truth prevails.

Love knows no limit to its endurance, no end to its trust, no fading of its hope; it can outlast anything. It is, in fact, the one thing that still stands when all else has fallen.

– 1 Corinthians 13:1–8 (Phillips)

LOVE IS THE VERY ESSENCE OF UNITY, SO I GUESS THAT'S THE SOUL-EXPOSING QUESTION:

HOW MUCH DO WE LOVE?

May God who is Love fill us with all His fullness, may He cause us to know the breadth and length and height and depth of Christ's love, may he root us and ground us in love, may He, who can do exceedingly abundantly more than we could ask or think to ask, be glorified forever and ever. Amen.

APPENDIX

THE ESSENTIAL DOCTRINES OF THE CHRISTIAN FAITH
ARTICLE ID: JAE100-1 | BY: NORMAN L. GEISLER

PART ONE

This article first appeared in the Christian Research Journal, volume 28, number 5 (2005). For further information or to subscribe to the Christian Research Journal go to: http://www.equip.org

SYNOPSIS

A historical approach to the topic of the essentials of the faith begins with the earliest creeds embedded in the New Testament and traces creedal development through the early forms of the Apostles Creed to the Nicene Creed and the Athanasian Creed. Unity among all major sections of Christendom is found in the statement: One Bible, two testaments, three confessions, four councils, and five centuries. From here there are divergent views, such as Eastern Orthodoxy's acceptance of seven general church councils and Roman Catholicism's acceptance of twenty-one. Anabaptists reject the authority of any church council but accept in general the doctrines that were declared at the first four councils, based on their belief in sola scriptura (the Bible alone).

The essential doctrines of the Christian faith that emerge from this historical approach are those contained in the Apostles Creed and unfolded in subsequent creeds of the first five centuries. These include (1)human depravity, (2)Christ's virgin birth, (3)Christ's sinlessness, (4)Christ's deity, (5)Christ's humanity, (6)God's unity, (7)God's triunity, (8)the necessity of God's grace, (9)the necessity of faith, (10) Christ's atoning death, (11)Christ's bodily resurrection, (12)Christ's bodily ascension, (13)Christ's present High Priestly service, and (14)

Christ's second coming, final judgment, and reign. Heaven and hell are implied in the final judgment and are explicated in later creeds. The ancient dictum in essentials, unity; in non-essentials, liberty; and in all things, charity resonates with practically everyone. The question is, What are the essentials? There are three main reasons for seeking the answer to this. First, the essential doctrines are the basis for our unity, since true unity is unity in the truth, and these doctrines are the essential truths. Second, the essential doctrines distinguish cults of Christianity from true Christianity, since these groups claim to be Christian but deny one or more of the essential doctrines of the historic Christian Church. It is not possible to identify these cults, however, unless we know what the essentials are. Third, the essential doctrines are the only truths over which we rightly can divide (i.e., break fellowship). It is better to be divided over truth than to be united in error where essentials are concerned (e.g., Gal. 1:6-9; 2:11-14; 1 Tim. 1:19-20; Titus 1:9; 1 John 2:19), but it is a great error for those who hold the truth to be divided where non-essentials are concerned (e.g., Eph. 4:3). It behooves us, therefore, to know the difference; otherwise, we may find ourselves dividing from those with whom we should be united and uniting with those from whom we should be divided.

Fortunately, we are not the first to tread this ground. The church, particularly the early church, has faced this issue before. It will be helpful, therefore, to look at some historic attempts to define the core Christian beliefs before we attempt to spell out what these essentials may be. With St. Augustine, we can thank God for heretics[6], for without them the church would not have been forced to clarify what was resident in the original deposit of faith.

HISTORIC EXPRESSIONS OF ESSENTIAL DOCTRINES

Many of the New Testament books and creed-like statements in them arose from a context of heretical denials of truths that were contained in the unfolding Christian revelation. There are several of these short creed-like confessions. One is found in 1 Timothy 3:16:

---

6   Augustine, *Of True Religion, Augustine: Earlier Writings*, ed. J.H.S.Burleigh (Philadelphia: Westminster, 1953),8.

God was manifested in the flesh, Justified in the Spirit, Seen by angels, Preached among the Gentiles, Believed on in the world, Received up in glory.[7]

Some believe that this passage is the core of what later became the Apostles[nkp22] Creed. It contains (1)the deity of Christ, (2)His incarnation (humanity), (3)His resurrection, (4)His proclamation and reception, and (5)His ascension. Brief and important as it is, however, there is no reason to believe that it was intended to state all of the essentials of the Christian faith. It, nonetheless, expresses core Christian doctrines.

Another creed-like statement is found in 1 Corinthians 15:35. The confession that is repeated several times:

That Christ died for our sins according to the Scriptures, and that He was buried, and that He rose again the third day according to the Scriptures, and that He was seen by Cephas [Peter], then by the twelve.

Here, too, the essentials of the gospel (v.1) are preserved, but there is no reason to believe that these are all the fundamental Christian doctrines. Nonetheless, the foundation in the inspired Scriptures, the death and burial of our Lord, and His physical bodily resurrection and appearances are all essentials of the Christian faith, as are the doctrines that we are sinners and that Christ died for sinners.

Peters Kerygma in Acts 10

Others point to the kerygma (proclamation) of Peter as the confessional core of New Testament Christianity. The outline of this is said to be in Peter's sermon in Acts 10:36-43[nkp25]: The word which God sent to the children of Israel, preaching peace through Jesus Christ [1]He is Lord of all that word you know, which was proclaimed throughout all Judea, and starting from Galilee after the baptism which John preached: how [2]God anointed Jesus of Nazareth with the Holy Spirit and with power, who went about doing good and healing all who were oppressed by the devil, for God was with Him. [3]And we are witnesses of all things which he did both in the land of the Jews and in Jerusalem, whom [4]they killed by hanging on

---

7   All Bible quotations are from the New King James Version.

a tree. [5]Him God raised up on the third day, [6]and showed him openly, not to all the people, but to witnesses chosen before by God, even to us who ate and drank with Him after He arose from the dead. And He commanded us to preach to the people, and to testify that it is [7]He who was ordained by God to be Judge of the living and the dead. To Him all the prophets witness that, through His name, [8]whoever believes in Him will receive remission of sins.

It has been observed that this kerygmatic paragraph contains the outline of the gospel of Mark, which many consider to be Peter's gospel, since Mark was his assistant (1 Pet. 5:13) and perhaps helped Peter in its composition. The essential doctrines of the Christian faith that it mentions (numbered above) are (1)the deity of Christ, (2) the deity and personality of the Holy Spirit, (3)the apostolic witness, (4)the humanity and death of Christ, (5)His bodily resurrection, (6) His bodily appearances, (7)His second coming and final judgment following, and (8)salvation by faith in Christ.

Some scholars believe that a treatise on this topic existed in the early church, although only a few fragments survive. Clement of Alexandria apparently had a copy of it, and Origen thought it was genuine in whole or in part.[8]

The Apostles'[nkp27] Creed

One of the first attempts at a formal Christian creed to be preserved as such is known as the Apostles'[nkp28] Creed. It underwent several changes throughout the early centuries of the church.

The Old Roman Creed. The earliest form of the Apostles'[nkp29] Creed came into existence in Rome:

> I believe in God Almighty, and in Christ Jesus, His only Son, our Lord; who was born of the Holy Spirit and the Virgin Mary; who was crucified under Pontius Pilate and was buried, and the third day rose from the dead; who ascended into heaven, and sitteth on the right hand of the Father, whence he cometh to judge the living and the dead. And in the Holy Ghost, the holy church, the remission of sins, the resurrection of the flesh, the life everlasting.

---

8   *The Oxford Dictionary of the Christian Church*, ed. F.L.Cross, 2nd ed. (Oxford University Press, 1978),1070.

The Gallican Creed. By the sixth century, certain changes had occurred in the Apostles'[nkp30] Creed. This version reads as follows (with significant changes indicated in italics):

> I believe in God *the Father* Almighty. I also believe in Jesus Christ His only Son, our Lord, *conceived of the Holy Spirit, born of the Virgin Mary, suffered* under Pontius Pilate, crucified, *dead* and buried; *He descended into hell,* rose again the third day, ascended into heaven, sat down at the right hand of the Father, thence He is to come to judge the living and the dead. I believe in the Holy Ghost, the holy *catholic* church, *the communion of saints,* the remission of sins, the resurrection of the flesh and life eternal.

The most crucial additions were that Jesus suffered (which contradicted the views of Docetism that denied His real humanity and hence His ability to suffer), that He descended into hell (which acknowledged its existence), and the addition of the words catholic (meaning universal) and communion (indicating a general unity of believers around this common doctrinal core).

The essential doctrines contained in this version include (1)the Trinity, (2)the deity of Christ, (3)His virgin conception, (4) His humanity, (5)His suffering and death for our sins, (6)His physical resurrection, (7)His present position at the Fathers[nkp31] right hand, and (8)His second coming and final judgment. Throughout the creed, of course, is (9)the necessity to believe in order to have remission of sins, for it begins with I believe.[nkp32]

The Current Creed. The current form of the Apostles'[nkp33] Creed did not take shape until about AD 750[9]. It differs little in substance from the Gallican Creed. The most significant difference is the added statement about creation (indicated in italics):

> I believe in God, the Father Almighty, *the Creator of heaven and earth,* and in Jesus Christ, His only Son, our Lord; who was conceived of the Holy Spirit, born of the Virgin Mary, suffered under Pontius Pilate, was crucified, died, and was buried. He descended into hell. The third day He arose again

---

9   *Documents of the Christian Church,* ed. Henry Bettenson (New York and London: Oxford University Press, 1961),35

from the dead. He ascended into heaven and sits at the right hand of God the Father Almighty, whence He shall come to judge the living and the dead. I believe in the Holy Spirit, the holy catholic church, the communion of saints, the forgiveness of sins, the resurrection of the flesh [Gk. sarx], and life everlasting.

The use of the word body instead of flesh, as is found in many recent translations of the Apostles'[nkp34] Creed, is an important change with doctrinal implications. The Greek word sarx[nkp35] in the Apostles'[nkp36] Creed was properly translated as flesh up until modern times. It has been replaced by the word body, which gives way more easily to a denial of the physical nature of the resurrection. This is due to neo-Gnostic influences on contemporary Christianity manifested in neo-orthodoxy[10] and some neo-evangelical beliefs[11].

The Nicene Creed (AD 325)

The second great creed amplified the expression of orthodoxy to counter heresies that denied the deity of Christ, His coequal status with the Father, and His being of one substance (essence) with the Father. It also was changed.

The Original Creed. The original AD325 version states (with significant additions to the Apostles'[nkp37] Creed indicated in italics):

We believe in one God the Father Almighty, Maker of heaven and earth, and of all things visible and invisible. And in one Lord Jesus Christ, the *only-begotten* Son of God, *begotten of the Father, Light of Light, Very God of Very God, begotten, not made, being of one substance with the Father by whom all things were made; who for us men, and for our salvation, came down and was incarnate and was made man;* He suffered, and the third day He rose again, ascended into heaven; from thence He shall come to judge the quick [living] and the dead. And [we believe] in the Holy Ghost.

---

10 See NormanL.Geisler, *The Battle for the Resurrection* (Nashville: Thomas Nelson Publishers, 1989), chap.6.

11 The neo-orthodox theologian Emil Brunner declared emphatically, Resurrection of the body, yes: Resurrection of the flesh, no! See Dogmatics, vol. 2, *The Christian Doctrine of Creation and Redemption* (Philadelphia: Westminster Press, 1952),372.

The Constantinopolitan Creed. The enlarged, Constantinople version of AD381 reads (with significant changes indicated in italics):

> We believe in one God the Father Almighty, Maker of heaven and earth, and of all things visible and invisible. And in one Lord Jesus Christ, the only-begotten Son of God, begotten of the *Father before all worlds, God of God,* Light of Light, Very God of Very God, begotten, not made, being of one substance with the Father by whom all things were made; who for us men, and for our salvation, *came down from heaven,* and was incarnate *by the Holy Spirit of the Virgin Mary,* and was made man, and *was crucified also for us under Pontius Pilate.* He suffered *and was buried,* and the third day He rose again *according to the Scriptures,* and ascended into heaven, and *sitteth on the right hand of the Father.* And He shall come *again with glory* to judge *both* the quick and the dead, *whose kingdom shall have no end. And we believe in the Holy Spirit, the Lord and Giver of Life, who proceedeth from the Father, who with the Father and the Son together is worshipped and glorified, who spoke by the prophets. And we believe one holy catholic and apostolic church. We acknowledge one baptism for the remission of sins. And we look for the resurrection of the dead, and the life of the world to come.*

The significant additions to the Apostles' Creed include (1)a stress on Christs'[nkp38] full deity, (2)the oneness of the Godhead, (3)Christ's[nkp39] role in creation, (4)His true humanity and incarnation, (5)His mission to save us, (6)the glory of His return, (7) Christ's[nkp40] reign following His second coming, and (8)the procession of the Holy Spirit from the Father. The original version was careful to add that Christ was not made, that is, He was uncreated and eternal, Very God of Very God.

The most significant intramural debate among conservative theologians is that over the filioque clause (and the Son), which affirms that the Holy Spirit proceeds from the Son as well as from the Father. The phrase was not in the original Nicene Creed (AD325) but was added in AD589 at the non-ecumenical[nkp41] Third Council of Toledo. When it was adopted by the Roman Church, it became the occasion for the split of the Eastern Orthodox Church from Rome in AD1050[12]. In his classic work, Creeds of Christendom, historian Philip Schaff concurs with this account, adding that the present text of the Apostles'[nkp42] Creed as a complete whole, we can hardly trace beyond the sixth, certainly not beyond the close of the fifth century, and its triumph over all the other forms in the Latin Church was not completed till the eighth century[13].

The Nicene Creed was, as Schaff asserts, the first which obtained universal authority in the Christian church[14]; but even so, it had three forms: the original Nicene (AD325); the enlarged Constantinopolitan (AD381), which adds everything after we believe in the Holy Spirit except the anathema; and the still later Latin form when the filioque clause was approved (but not added to the creed) by popes LeoIII (AD809) and NicholasI (AD858)[15]. This papal approval eventually led to the phrase being added to the creed, and to the split with the Eastern Church.

The Athanasian Creed (c. AD428 or later)[16]. Most scholars no longer believe that Athanasius authored this creed; nevertheless, it does reflect his strong emphasis on the deity of Christ. It also is the earliest and strongest explicit creedal statement on the Trinity. The Anglicans and most Protestant bodies, consequently, adopted it, though some have had reservations about the condemnation to hell on all who reject the truth of the incarnation and the Trinity. It reads as follows:

> Whoever will be saved, before all things it is necessary that he hold the catholic faith. Which faith except every one do keep whole and undefiled, without doubt he shall perish everlastingly. And the catholic faith is this: that we worship one God in Trinity, and Trinity in unity; neither confounding the persons, nor dividing the substance [essence]. For there is one person of the Father, another of the Son, and another

---

12   *The Oxford Dictionary*, 51213.

13   Philip Schaff, *The Creeds of Christendom: The History of the Creeds* (Grand Rapids: Baker Book House, 1983),1.19.

14   Ibid., 24

15   See Schaff, 1.26.

16   Philip Schaff claims it is a clear and precise summary of the doctrinal decisions of the first four ecumenical Councils between AD 325 and 451 (*The Creeds of Christendom*, 1.37). This would place it after AD451.

of the Holy Ghost. But the Godhead of the Father, of the Son, and of the Holy Ghost, is all one: the glory equal, the majesty coeternal[nkp43].The Father [is] uncreate[d], the Son [is] uncreate[d], and the Holy Ghost [is] uncreate[d].So the Father is God, the Son is God, and the Holy Spirit is God.So[nkp44] are we forbidden by the catholic religion to say, there be three Gods, or three Lords. The Father is made of none: neither created, nor begotten. The Son is of the Father alone: not made, nor created, but begotten.And[nkp45] in the Trinity none is before, or after another: none is greater, or less than another. But the whole three persons are coeternal[nkp46], and coequal[nkp47].He[nkp48] therefore that will be saved must thus think of the Trinity. Furthermore, it is necessary to everlasting salvation that he also believe rightly the incarnation of our Lord Jesus Christ. For the right faith is, that we believe and confess: that our Lord Jesus Christ, the Son of God, is God and man; God, of the substance [essence] of the Father; begotten before the worlds; and man, of the substance [essence] of his mother, born in the world; perfect God, and perfect man; of a reasonable soul and human flesh subsisting. Equal to the Father, as touching His Godhead; and inferior to the Father, as touching His manhood. Who although He be God and man; yet He is not two, but one Christ. One; not by conversion of the Godhead into flesh, but by taking of the manhood into God. One altogether; not confusion of substance [essence], but by unity of person.Who[nkp49] suffered for our salvation, descended into hell, rose again the third day from the dead. He ascended into heaven; He sitteth on the right hand of the Father, God Almighty. From thence He shall come to judge the quick and the dead. At whose coming all men shall rise again with their bodies, and shall give account of their works. And they that have done good shall go into life everlasting; and they that have done evil into everlasting fire.

Several things in this creed demand attention. First, the emphasis is on the Trinity and the incarnation of Christ. Second, the framers strongly believed not only that orthodox doctrine is important, but that it is necessary for salvation. Third, the creed is directed against many heresies: Against tritheism, it affirms there are not three Gods, but one God. Against Monophysitism, it asserts that there is no confusion or commingling[nkp50] of Christ's[nkp51] two natures (human and divine). Against Nestorianism, it declares that there is a unity of Christ's[nkp52] two natures in one person. Against Arianism, it declares that the Son is coequal in substance with the Father and was not made but is uncreated and eternal. In response to the logically absurd notion that the infinite God became a finite human, it makes it clear that deity did not become humanity, but that the second person of the Godhead assumed a human nature in addition to His divine nature. This, of course, eliminates the heresy of adoptionism, that Jesus was merely a man who was adopted into the Godhead as Son. It was not the subtraction of deity, but the addition of humanity. It also excludes Appolinarianism, since it refers to the Son being fully human, a perfect man, of a reasonable soul and human flesh subsisting, not partially human. Finally, this is the first of the creeds to explicitly address the nature of the final judgment after Christ's[nkp53] second coming as everlasting life (heaven) for the saved and everlasting fire (hell) for the lost. Everlasting life entails conscious existence, therefore, so does the parallel phrase everlasting fire. The phrase perish everlastingly also implies consciousness, since in annihilation one would perish instantly, not everlastingly. The creed, thus, also pronounces annihilationism as heretical; and since it implies that there will be people in both places, it excludes universalism from orthodoxy as well. In short, this is an amazing creed that explicitly anathematizes (pronounces as accursed) a great many heresies.

The Creed of Chalcedon (AD 451)

The third of the three great creeds is that of Chalcedon. It was adopted in an ecumenical session. It embraces the preceding creeds and adds to the unfolding theological essentials (additions are indicated in italics):

> Following, then, the holy fathers, we unite in teaching all men to confess the one and only Son, our Lord Jesus Christ. *This selfsame one is perfect both in deity and in humanness;* this selfsame one is also actually God and actually man, *with a rational [human] soul and a body.* He is of *the same reality as God* as far as His deity is concerned and of *the same reality as we ourselves* as far as His humanness is concerned; thus

like us in all respects, sin only excepted. *Before time began he was begotten of the Father,* in respect of His deity, and now in these last days, for us and behalf of[nkp54] our salvation, this selfsame one was born of Mary the virgin, *who is God-bearer in respect of His humanness.* We also teach that we apprehend this one and only Christ-Son, Lord, only-begotten in[nkp55] two natures; and we do this without confusing *the two natures, without transmuting [changing] one nature into the other, without dividing them into two separate categories,* without contrasting them according to area or function. *The distinctiveness of each nature is not nullified by the union.* Instead, the properties of each nature are conserved *and both natures concur in one person and in one reality [hypostasis]. They are not divided or cut into two persons, but are together the one and only and only-begotten Word [Logos]* of God, the Lord Jesus Christ. Thus have the prophets of old testified; thus the Lord Jesus Christ Himself taught us; thus the symbol of fathers [i.e., the Nicene Creed] has handed down to us.

In addition to the triune Godhead, the virgin birth of Christ, and His humanity and deity, this creed stresses the hypostatic unity of His two natures in one person (thus opposing Nestorianism and Monophysitism), without separation or confusion. The perfection and completion of both natures also is emphasized, along with the eternality of the Son, before all time. In addition, with the accent on the union of the two natures, the creed goes so far as to call Mary the God-bearer (Gk. theotokos), because the person she gave birth to with regard to His human nature was also God with regard to His divine nature.

DISCERNING CRITERIA FOR ORTHODOXY

With this historical context in place, we are better prepared to discern just what the essentials of the Christian faith are. A historical analysis does not solve all the problems, however, since not all sections of Christendom accept all the creeds and councils of the church. Most sections of Christendom accept the first three creeds (Apostles'[nkp56], Nicene, and Chalcedon) and four councils (Nicaea, Constantinople, Ephesus, and Chalcedon) as a definitive statement of orthodoxy; however, not all do.

The Roman Catholic View

Roman Catholics accept twenty-one church councils as authoritative. Eastern Orthodox, however, accept only the first seven as authoritative, and all non-Catholics reject the authority of the later councils, pointing to numerous doctrines pronounced in them that are contrary to Scripture. These include worshiping icons, venerating Mary, praying for the dead, purgatory, the necessity of works for salvation, the inspiration of the Apocrypha, the worship of the consecrated communion elements, the bodily assumption of Mary, and the infallibility of the pope[17].

The Reformed View

Reformed view here refers to what is known as the Magisterial Reformation (following Luther and Calvin). This tradition generally accepts the doctrines of only the first four church councils, since beginning with the fifth council objectionable doctrines began to emerge. Those in this Reformed tradition, nevertheless, agree with the other major sections of Christendom on the dictum: One Bible, two testaments, three creeds, four councils, and five centuries.

In general, if one considers only the major doctrines in these creeds, and not the anathemas or the question of their authority, even most of the rest of Christendom (namely, the Anabaptists) agree with their basic doctrinal expression of the Christian faith. There are, however, three important qualifications. First, there is the issue of the anathemas. Most evangelicals would not agree that those who deny any one of the doctrines in the Athanasian Creed will go to hell, but this is what the creed says, namely: This is the catholic [i.e., universal] faith: which except a man believe faithfully, he can not be saved. A large section of evangelicalism denies that one must believe all of the doctrines as a condition for salvation.

Second, the creed appears to include baptismal regeneration[18] as one of the doctrines that is part of the orthodox creed to which one must agree or be lost forever. Both Calvin and the Anabaptists reject

---

17   See NormanL.Geisler and Ralph MacKenzie, *Roman Catholics and Evangelicals: Agreements and Differences* (Grand Rapids: Baker Book House, 1995).

18   For an in-depth discussion of baptismal regeneration, see H. Wayne House, *Baptism for The Forgiveness of Sins: Sign, Seal, or Means of Grace?* Part One, Christian Research Journal 22, 2 (1999): 26ff, and Part Two, Christian Research Journal 22,3 (2000):22ff (http://www.equip.org/free/DB055-1.htm and http://www.equip,org/free/DB055-2.htm).

baptismal regeneration, and even most people who accept the doctrine would not agree that those who reject it will go to hell forever.

Finally, the Athanasian Creed appears to affirm the amillennial view adopted by the later Augustine and many who followed him, whereas many of the early church fathers before him and even Augustine himself in his earlier period were premillennial[19]. The creed seems to declare one general resurrection of both saved and lost when Christ returns, whereas the premillennial view calls for two resurrections separated by a thousand years (cf. Rev.20:46[nkp57]). Even most who are amillennial, however, would not make this doctrine a test of orthodoxy, as indeed it should not be.

The Anabaptist View

This view is sometimes called the Radical Reformation[20]. Most Baptist, Congregationalist, Charismatic, Mennonite, Free Church, and Independent Church traditions come from this tradition. Many in this tradition had great respect for the Apostles'[nkp58] Creed and were evangelical in their central doctrinal beliefs, but they rejected any ecclesiastical authority, holding strongly to the view that the Bible alone has divine authority. This did not mean that they believed that confessions had no value, or that the early creeds did not contain essential orthodox doctrine. It simply means that they believed that only the Bible is infallible and divinely authoritative. In the words of Thomas Aquinas (AD 12251274[nkp59]), who summed up the belief of many Fathers before him, We believe the successors of the apostles only in so far as they tell us those things which the apostles and prophets have left in their writings[nkp60].[21]

---

19   Early fathers[nkp61] patristic works that were premillennial include Barnabas, Clement of Rome, Shepherd of Hermas, Ignatius, Polycarp, Papias, Irenaeus, Commodianus, Justin Martyr, Lactantius, Methodius, Epiphaius, Gregory of Myssa, and the Testament of the Twelve Patriarchs. See George Peters, *The Theocratic Kingdom* (Grand Rapids: Kregel Books, 1972 reprint), 1.451. For Augustines[nkp62] earlier position, see City of God,20.7.

20   See George Hunston Williams, The Radical Reformation (Truman State University Press, 2000) and Leonard Verduin, *The Reformers and Their Stepchildren* (Grand Rapids: Eerdmans,1964).

21   Aquinas, On Truth,14.1011.

PART TWO

This article first appeared in the Christian Research Journal, volume28, number6 (2005). For further information or to subscribe to the Christian Research Journal go to: http://www.equip.org

SYNOPSIS

Part two in this series takes a logical approach to answering the question of what makes a doctrine essential. There are two criteria: First, the doctrine must concern and be connected to our salvation; that is, it must be salvific. Second, its connection to our salvation must be crucial; that is, it must be so tied to our salvation that if it were not true, our salvation as God revealed it would not be possible. When these criteria are applied to the list discovered by the historical approach outlined in part one, the same basic doctrines emerge. The Trinity, the deity of Christ, His atoning death, and His bodily resurrection are all necessary in the first stage of salvation: justification (salvation from the penalty of sin in the past). Christ's ascension and present advocacy are necessary in the second stage: sanctification (salvation from the power of sin in the present). Christ's second coming and final judgments are necessary in the third stage: glorification (salvation from the presence of sin in the future). Christ's virgin birth is connected to salvation because it speaks of His sinlessness and supernatural origin, which are necessary for salvation. The infallibility of the Bible is an essential doctrine in that by it we know the salvific doctrines, because those doctrines are based on the Scriptures.

These essential doctrines must necessarily be true to make salvation possible, but a person need not believe all of them to be saved. One, however, cannot deny certain of these doctrines, such as Christ's deity, His death for our sins, and His resurrection, and be saved.

Finally, the discussion of essential doctrines raises the question of whether Roman Catholicism is orthodox. If judged by historical standards, it is orthodox, because it affirms all of the doctrines in the creeds and councils of the first five centuries of the church. If judged by logical standards, however, it is unorthodox, because it denies those doctrines that the Protestant Reformers deemed to be essential to salvation, such as justification by grace alone through faith alone.

What are the essential doctrines of the Christian faith? One way to answer this question, as noted in part one of this series, is to take a historical approach: the essential doctrines are those found in the early creeds of the church. Another way to answer this is to take a logical approach. This approach is better, since it avoids many of the pitfalls of the historical approach, especially the debate about which creeds and councils should be accepted.

The logical approach simply begins with the teachings of the New Testament on salvation and asks, What are the essential doctrines on salvation without which salvation would not be possible? This approach yields the same basic salvation doctrines of the early creeds discussed in part one, except for the anathemas (curses for believing false doctrine)and baptismal regeneration. Salvation as described in the Bible, based in the deity, death, and resurrection of Christ—which is the gospel (1 Cor.15:1-6)—entails all these essential doctrines, including: (1)human depravity, (2)Christ's virgin birth, (3) Christ's sinlessness, (4)Christ's deity, (5)Christ's humanity, (6)God's unity, (7)God's triunity, (8)the necessity of God's grace, (9)the necessity of faith, (10)Christ's atoning death, (11)Christ's bodily resurrection, (12)Christ's bodily ascension, (13)Christ's present high priestly service, (14)Christ's second coming, final judgment, and reign.

Some may question how Christ's present service, second coming, kingdom reign, and final judgment are essential doctrines of salvation. The answer lies in understanding salvation in the broad sense of all three stages: justification, sanctification, and glorification. According to Scripture, (1)we have been saved from the penalty of sin (by justification)the moment we believe (Rom.3:28; 5:1; Gal.3:24), (2)we presently are in the process of being saved from the power of sin (by sanctification)(John 17:17; Eph. 5:25-26; 1 Thess.5:23), and (3)we will at death or at Christ's coming be saved from the very presence of sin (by glorification; that is, by being made perfect) (Rom. 8:30; 1 Cor.13:10-13; 1 John 3:2).

This being the case, we can see that doctrines 1-11 are essential for justification; that is, without them our justification would not be possible. Likewise, doctrines 12 and 13 (Christ's ascension and present service) are necessary for our sanctification, and doctrine 14 (the second coming) is needed to complete salvation, namely, to achieve our glorification.[22] These last three doctrines (12–14) are not always given in lists of essentials of the faith because in such cases only the doctrines regarding our justification are in view.[23]

WHAT MAKES A DOCTRINE ESSENTIAL?

There are many important teachings of Scripture (e.g., the prohibitions against blasphemy, idolatry, adultery, and murder)that are not among the previously listed doctrines. What, then, makes a doctrine essential? Judging by the doctrines that the historic Christian church pronounced as essential, two basic characteristics emerge. First, the doctrine must be connected to our salvation. That is, it must be soteriological or salvific in nature. Second, its connection to our salvation must be crucial. In other words, salvation as God has revealed it would not be possible without the doctrine being true.

These two criteria are clearly revealed in most of the doctrines that were listed previously. The Trinity, Christ's deity, His atoning death, and His bodily resurrection are all necessary for our salvation. Further, as was shown earlier, Christ's ascension, present service, and second coming are necessary for salvation in the broad sense that includes not only justification but also sanctification and glorification. There are, however, other doctrines in the list that do not appear to be necessary for our salvation.

What about Christ's virgin birth (more precisely, His supernatural conception in the virgin Mary by the Holy Spirit)? Was it essential for our salvation? Certainly the underlying doctrine to which the virgin birth points—the sinlessness of Christ—is essential to salvation, for a sinner cannot be the Savior of other sinners.[24] He

---

22   The precise order of end-time events (pre-, a-, or post-millennial views)has never been made a test of creedal orthodoxy. The doctrine that the second coming and resurrection are future events is part of orthodoxy; hence, an extreme preterist view that denies these is unorthodox.

23   For further discussion of this point see Norman L. Geisler, Systematic Theology, vol.3, Sin, and Salvation (Grand Rapids: Bethany House Publishers, 2004), chap.17.

24   Precisely how the virgin birth prevented Christ from inheriting Adam's sinful nature is debated among scholars. The precise mechanism remains a mystery—at least to me. Several possibilities have been suggested, but none have gained universal acceptance. Two things seem clear as parameters of a viable explanation. It must have been something that preserved the genetic connection of Christ with Adam (which a virgin birth does through Mary, Christ's natural mother), whose race Christ was representing and saving (cf. Luke3:38; Rom.5:12–21;1 Cor.15:45; Gal.4:4;1 Kings8:19), and yet it must also be something that does not involve a natural generation of male and

would need a Savior himself. A drowning person can't save another drowning person. Was the virgin birth necessary, however, to Christ's being sinless? This much seems certain: anyone born the natural way would have been—short of divine intervention—a sinner like the rest of us (Rom.3:23;5:12); and the virgin birth (i.e., supernatural conception) was one way to circumvent this. Whether it was the only way or whether, say, an immaculate conception, whereby Christ would have been conceived in the natural way but without the stain of original sin, would have worked is both moot and irrelevant. The virgin birth was one way to do it, and it was the way God chose to do it. In addition, it was important, if not crucial, to our salvation that God supernaturally signify which of all the persons born of women (Gen.3:15; Gal.4:4) was His Son, the Savior of the world.[25] A natural but sinless conception of Christ would not have been an outward "sign" that drew attention to the Savior's supernatural and sinless nature from the very beginning. The virgin birth, therefore, was a divinely appointed necessity for our salvation, by the underlying doctrine of Christ's sinlessness and by the supernatural nature of it.

What is more, some have noted that the virgin birth points to and preserves the eternal Father-Son relationship between the first and second persons of the Trinity. While this does not explain in itself how Adam's sinful nature is transmitted to his natural posterity, it does offer a possible explanation for why the Adamic nature was not transmitted to Christ: Christ had no earthly father, only a heavenly one, who like Himself was sinless. By Christ's virgin birth the sinless heavenly Father-Son relationship was preserved and the earthly father-son relationship was interrupted; thus, neither Adam's sin, nor its consequence, death (Rom.5:12), could be transmitted to Christ. It was as impossible that the sinless Son could be born sinful as it was that the Prince of Life could be held by death (Acts 2:24; 3:15).[26]

---

female, which is the way we inherit Adam's fallen nature. These parameters would appear to eliminate several explanations that have been offered, namely: (1)that the sin nature is passed on only through the father's genes, although the mother has fallen genes as well, and (2)that God directly created a new sinless nature (not genetically connected to Adam) in Mary's womb as opposed to supernaturally fertilizing an ovum of Mary.

25 See J. Gresham Machen, *The Virgin Birth of Christ* (New York: Harper & Brothers, 1930).

26 For this point I am indebted to my friend and editor, Elliot Miller.

THE DIFFERENT KINDS OF ESSENTIALS

There are other reasons why one sees different lists of essential (or fundamental)doctrines of the faith. One reason is because of the failure to distinguish between three different kinds of essential doctrines: soteriological, epistemological, and hermeneutical.

Soteriological Essentials

Soteriological essentials are those having to do with salvation (Gk. soteria means "salvation"). In short, if these doctrines are not true, then salvation is not possible. This is why they are essentials of the faith, as the foregoing discussion shows.

As we've seen, soteriological essentials may be divided into those necessary for our justification (e.g., Christ's death and resurrection), those necessary for our sanctification (e.g., Christ's ascension and present session as our advocate), and those necessary for our glorification (e.g., His second coming and final judgment).

Epistemological Essentials

Conspicuous by its absence from the previous list of essentials is the inspiration of Scripture, which was listed as one of the great fundamentals of the faith by modern conservatives such as B. B. Warfield, Charles Hodge, and J. Gresham Machen. The reason for this omission is that the previous list contains only soteriological essentials. One can be saved without believing in the inspiration and (consequent)inerrancy of the Bible.[27] An inerrant Scripture is not necessary for salvation. People were saved before there was a Bible, and people are saved through reading errant copies of the Bible (as opposed to the inerrant original manuscripts). Further, belief in inerrancy is not necessary in order to be saved. Inspiration and inerrancy are not a test for evangelical authenticity, but for evangelical consistency. Inspiration and inerrancy are not part of the plan of salvation one must believe to be saved, but they are part of the foundation that makes that plan of salvation knowable. In order for us to have a sure foundation for what we believe, God deemed it necessary to provide an inerrant Word as the basis of our beliefs.

Inspiration, therefore, is not a soteriological essential; rather, it is an epistemological essential. Epistemology (Gk. episteme means

---

27   Inerrancy follows logically from divine inspiration; for if the Bible is the Word of God and God cannot err, then it follows logically that the Bible cannot err in anything it affirms (or denies).

"knowledge") deals with how we know. We never could be sure of the doctrines that are necessary for our salvation without a completely true, divinely authoritative revelation from God, such as we have in the Scriptures. The great ecumenical creeds, nonetheless, do mention "the Scriptures" as being the basis for what we believe; therefore, they do acknowledge this epistemological essential of the faith.

Hermeneutical Essentials

A third kind of essential is presupposed in this whole discussion: a hermeneutical essential (Gk. *hermencia* means "interpretation"). All of the previously mentioned doctrines relating to our salvation are based on a literal, historical-grammatical interpretation of Scripture.[28] Without this, there is no orthodoxy. Most cults specialize in denying this literal method of interpretation in part or in whole. This is how they so easily can twist Scripture to their own heretical advantage.[29]

The whole Protestant doctrine of sola scriptura ("Scripture alone") is based on the precondition of a literal interpretation of the Bible.[30] The literal hermeneutic is, therefore, the fundamental method that makes possible our knowledge of all the doctrinal essentials.

THE DIFFERENCE BETWEEN EXPLICIT AND IMPLICIT

Not all the essential doctrines in the creeds are stated explicitly. The doctrine of Scripture is one example. It is everywhere implied as the only infallible basis for Christian belief; however, it is nowhere treated explicitly. No creed or council ever treated it, but all of them implied it and cited it.

The doctrine of human depravity, likewise, is not explicitly treated in all these early creeds. It is, however, implied in the statements about Christ dying for our "sins" and about our need for "remission" and "forgiveness" of sins.

---

28 See Norman L. Geisler, *Systematic Theology, vol.4*, Church, Last Things (Grand Rapids: Bethany House Publishers, 2005), chap.13.

29 See Norman L. Geisler and Ron Rhodes, *Correcting the Cults: Expert Responses to Their Scripture Twisting* (Grand Rapids: Baker Books, 2005).

30 The "literal" method does not mean there can be no figures of speech. It means that the whole Bible is literally true, just as the author meant it, even though not everything in it is true literally. There are parables, metaphors, and many figures of speech in the Bible—all of which convey a literal truth.

It is this distinction between explicit and implicit doctrinal truth that has led many theologians to speak of fidei implicitus ("implicit faith"). For example, a person who believes in the deity of Christ and the oneness of God is implicitly a Trinitarian, even though he (or she)does not explicitly believe (because he is yet untaught) the formal doctrine of the Trinity. It would seem that such a person who believes the gospel (that the Lord Jesus Christ died for our sins and was resurrected) can be saved without yet being an explicit Trinitarian.

THE DIFFERENCE BETWEEN WHAT MUST BE TRUE AND TRUE AND WHAT MUST BE BELIEVED

Not all soteriological essentials are necessary to be believed in order to be saved. For example, the virgin birth is nowhere stated as part of what is necessary to be believed in order to be saved; nonetheless, if Jesus were not actually born of a virgin, then He would have been sinful like the rest of the natural-born sons of Adam (Rom.5:12f); and if He were sinful, then He could not be our Savior from sin. There is, therefore, a distinct difference between what must be true in order for us to be saved and what must be believed in order to be saved.

Someone, likewise, could not believe, or even could disbelieve, in the second coming of Christ and still be saved. If there were no second coming, however, then he could not be saved in the complete sense of some day being saved from the very presence of sin (glorification).

THE DIFFERENCE BETWEEEN DENIAL AND DISBELIEF

There are certain essential doctrines that a person may not believe and still be saved. He may not believe in the virgin birth, the inspiration of Scripture, the ascension of Christ, His advocacy before the Father, or His second coming, and still be saved. He may not believe them because he does not even know about them; or, he may know them and still not believe them.

There are, however, certain things that a person cannot deny today and still be saved.[31] He must believe the gospel—that Christ

---

31   We say "today" because in the progress of revelation God has ordained that more content be explicitly believed today (e.g., the "name" of Jesus—Acts 4:12; John 3:18; 3:36; 8:21) than in Old Testament times (cf. Gen.15:5–6; Jonah3). For more on the contents of salvation, see Geisler, Systematic Theology, vol.3, chap.17.

died for our sins and was resurrected (1 Cor.15:1–6). He must "believe on the Lord Jesus Christ" (Acts 16:31, emphasis added).[32] He must believe "in [his] heart that God has raised Him [Jesus] from the dead" (Rom.10:9). When "Lord" (Gk. kurios) is used of Christ in the New Testament it means, or refers to, His deity.[33] It follows, therefore, that one cannot deny the deity of Christ and be saved.

It is conceivable, however, that one who is uninformed of the deity of Christ could not believe it and still be saved. Certainly not all of the Old Testament saints who were saved understood and believed in the deity of the Messiah. It is not so, however, that one who is informed of the deity of Christ could not believe it and still be saved. There is no New Testament ground for affirming that those today who understand about Christ's deity and yet deny it are saved. It is now a normative and necessary condition for salvation (Rom. 10:9; Acts 2:21, 36; 3:14–16; 5:30–35; 10:39; 16:31; 1 Cor.12:3). One must "believe on the Lord Jesus Christ" to be saved (Acts 16:31, emphasis added). One must believe in his heart and confess with his mouth "the Lord Jesus" to be saved (Rom.10:9–10, emphasis added). This would mean that one who believes, as Jehovah's Witnesses do, that Jesus is Michael, a created angel, cannot be saved. Likewise, no one who believes, as Mormons do, that Jesus is the brother of Lucifer can be saved. This would also mean that any Arian (follower of the fourth century heretic Arius), who denies the deity of Christ, cannot be saved.[34]

THE DIFFERENCE BETWEEN HERESY AND SALVATION

One can believe heretical views on some doctrines, however, and still be saved. Being saved (justified) depends only on believing certain saving truths such as Christ's deity, His death for our sins, and His resurrection. One may disbelieve the virgin birth, inspiration of

---

32   All Bible quotations are from the New King James Version.

33   The word "Lord" (Gk. kurios) as used of Jesus in the New Testament clearly means deity because: (1)In the Greek Old Testament (the Septuagint)it is the common translation of the Hebrew word Yahweh ("Lord" in English translations), which only means God. (2)It is used in the New Testament (i.e., Greek) translation of Old Testament Scriptures that refer to Yahweh (e.g., Matt.3:3;22:44). (3)It is used in the context of worshiping Christ (e.g., John20:28; Phil.2:10), but God alone was worshiped.

34   It is possible that some Arians are not properly informed about the deity of Christ, having only an implicit faith in it, and still are saved. In this case, however, the proof that they have this implicit faith in it would be that when properly taught from Scripture about it, they would then place their faith in Christ's deity explicitly (cf. Acts 19:1–6).

the Bible, Christ's ascension, and second coming, however, and still be saved. In short, one can hold heretical views on a number of doctrines and still be saved. Such a person is, of course, unbiblical and inconsistent; but better to be inconsistently saved than consistently lost. It is, of course, better yet to be consistently saved, but that is not the question at hand.

THE DIFFERENCE BETWEEN PARTIALLY HERETICAL AND COMPLETELY HERETICAL

If a person denies one essential doctrine, does that make him a heretic? It makes him heretical on that particular doctrine he denies, but not heretical on everything else. For example, if one denies the inerrancy of the Bible, he can still be saved. Inerrancy, as epistemologically important as it is, is simply not part of the plan of salvation that is necessary to believe in order to be saved. One can, likewise, deny the virgin birth and still be saved for the same reasons. Being unorthodox on one doctrine does not mean a person is unorthodox on other doctrines. One must, of course, be orthodox on certain salvific doctrines in order to be saved.

WHAT ABOUT ROMAN CATHOLICISM?

When it comes to Roman Catholicism, there are really two questions. First, does Roman Catholicism contain salvific heresies? Second, can a Roman Catholic be saved by following official Catholic doctrine?

First, judged by the standards of the creeds and councils of the first five centuries, Roman Catholicism is orthodox. It does not deny any of the doctrines contained in the first four ecumenical councils. It affirms them all. If, however, it is judged by Reformation standards of sola fidei ("faith alone"), sola scriptura ("Scripture alone"), sola Christa ("Christ alone"), and sola gratia ("grace alone"), it is not orthodox.[35] The question is whether or not these Reformation teachings are the proper test for orthodoxy. Judged by the historic creedal standards, Roman Catholicism is a true church with significant error,

---

35   For further discussion on sola gratia, see Norman L. Geisler and Ralph MacKenzie, *Roman Catholics and Evangelicals: Agreements and Differences* (Grand Rapids: Baker Academic, 1995), part2.

not a false church with significant truth. Judged by Reformation standards, it is a false church with significant truth.[36]

Second, is the gospel contained in official Roman Catholic doctrine? Again, as defined by the norms of the Reformation, it would appear that the answer is no. Many Protestant theologians, in fact, believed that the Roman Catholic church officially apostatized at the Council of Trent (1545–1563) when it proclaimed, among other unbiblical teachings, that "if anyone shall say that the good works of the man justified are in such a way the gift of God that they are not also the good merits of him who is justified, or that the one justified by good works . . . does not truly merit increase of grace, eternal life, and the attainment of that eternal life (if he should die in grace), and also an increase in glory; let him be anathema."[37]

Roman Catholic theologians, however, are quick to point out several things. First, what Catholics call initial justification (and Protestants call justification) comes totally by God's grace and apart from any works, since it happens to a baby when he is baptized and thereby regenerated.[38] Further, even in adults salvation is totally dependent on the work of Christ on the cross, without which no one could be saved. Finally, even the good works believers perform are possible only by the grace of God. In short, Catholic doctrine teaches the absolute necessity of the finished work of Christ on the cross and of God's grace for our salvation. The new Catholic catechism states, "Our salvation comes from the grace of God" and even "the merits of our good works are gifts of the divine goodness."[39] Even Trent affirmed that "if anyone shall say that man can be justified

---

36 Among the significant errors of Rome are the addition of the Apocrypha to the Bible, the addition of works to faith as a condition for salvation, the addition of Mary to Christ as a Mediatrix of salvation, the addition of purgatory to the cross to pay for our complete salvation, the addition of prayers offered to dead creatures to prayers offered to the living God, and the addition of the worship of the consecrated host to the worship of the incarnate Christ.

37 Heinrich Denzinger, *The Sources of Catholic Dogma*, trans. Roy J. Defarrari (St. Louis: B. Herder Book Co., 1957), no.842,261.

38 If the Catholic view is called heretical because of infant baptism, then the Eastern Orthodox, Anglican, and Lutheran views must be called heretical for the same reason. This would mean that more than two thirds of Christendom holds a heretical view of justification.

39 Catechism of the Catholic Church (1994), 2009.

before God by his own works which are done . . . without divine grace through Christ Jesus: let him be anathema." Further, "nothing that precedes justification, whether faith or works, merits the grace of justification. For if it is by grace, it is no more of works."[40]

In summary, it would appear that there is enough truth inside official Roman Catholicism for those who believe it to be saved, at least by the historic standards for orthodoxy found in the early creeds and councils. It would seem to beg the question to impose the Reformation standards on the pre-Reformation church. This is not to say the Reformation was not right. It was. Salvation comes through faith alone, based on the work of Christ alone, provided by grace alone, grounded in the Word of God alone. Roman Catholicism obscured the essential saving truth of the gospel by overlaying it with error and contradicting it in practice.

THE LIST OF ESSENTIALS

The list of essential Christian doctrines that emerge from the early creeds and councils includes (1)human depravity, (2)Christ's virgin birth, (3)Christ's sinlessness, (4)Christ's deity, (5)Christ's humanity, (6)God's unity, (7)God's triunity, (8)the necessity of God's grace, (9)the necessity of faith, (10)Christ's atoning death, (11)Christ's bodily resurrection, (12)Christ's bodily ascension, (13)Christ's present high priestly service, and (14)Christ second coming, final judgment (heaven and hell), and reign. All of these are necessary for salvation to be possible in the broad sense, which includes justification, sanctification, and glorification.

It is not necessary, however, to believe all of these to be saved (justified). The minimum necessary to believe in order to be saved is: (1)human depravity, (3)Christ's sinlessness, (4)Christ's deity, (5) Christ's humanity, (6)God's unity, (7)God's triunity, (8)the necessity of God's grace, (9)the necessity of faith, (10)Christ's atoning death, and (11)Christ's bodily resurrection.

It is not necessary to believe in (2)Christ's virgin birth, (12)Christ's bodily ascension, (13)Christ's present service, or (14)Christ's second coming and final judgment as a condition for obtaining a right standing with God (justification). Even some of those beliefs that are necessary may be more implicit than explicit; for example, human depravity and God's triunity. Regarding human depravity, one must believe that he is a sinner in need of a Savior, but need not believe all that the orthodox doctrine of human depravity involves, such as the inheritance of a sin nature. The deity of Christ, likewise, is involved, which in turn involves at least two persons who are God (the Father and the Son); but there is no reason to think that to be saved one must understand and explicitly believe the orthodox doctrine of the personality and deity of the Holy Spirit who is united with those two persons in one nature (i.e., one God). Many people, in fact, do not understand this doctrine clearly, even years after they were saved.

All of the essential doctrines are necessary to make salvation possible, but not all are essential for one to believe in order for one to be saved. All are essential to believe to be a consistent[41] Christian, but not all are necessary to believe to become a Christian. Generally, a sign that authentic conversion has occurred is that when a professing believer is instructed on these doctrines, he embraces them.

This article reprinted with permission
Christian Research Journal Article: Norman L. Geisler, "The Essential Doctrines of the Christian Faith," ChristianResearch Journal 28, no. 6 (2005):

http://www.equip.org/articles/the-essential-doctrines-of-the-christian-faith-part-one/

http://www.equip.org/articles/the-essential-doctrines-of-the-christian-faith-part-two/

---

41   Consistent not only in a logical, theological sense, but also in a practical and spiritual sense.

ABOUT THE AUTHOR

Jim Turner is a husband and father of four. Mr. Turner has been in youth or pastoral ministry for over 25 years and has personally experienced the hurt and frustration that disagreement can cause. He has also counseled and mediated on numerous occasions where disagreement threatened to split churches and undo relationships that were years in the building. His experience includes churches from 10 to 1,000 members.

Mr. Turner's spiritual background includes his salvation experience while a student at Purdue University, West Lafayette, IN. Led to Christ through the ministry of Campus Crusade for Christ, Mr. Turner was faithfully discipled and challenged to live a life fully sold out to Christ. After two years of discipleship and steady spiritual growth many fellow believers encouraged him to pursue full time ministry. After much counsel and prayerful consideration Mr. Turner enrolled in the School of Religion at Bob Jones University, Greenville, SC, and graduated with a BA in Pastoral Studies and a minor in Public Speaking. He then went on to complete additional courses at Bob Jones Seminary.

Mr. Turner has also been a business owner for over 15 years in the area of sales and marketing. Mr. Turner has started and built four businesses from scratch with varying degrees of success. He has served the advertising needs of Fortune 500 companies all the way down to sole proprietors.

Mr. Turner's experience lends itself to promotion and practical ministry application of his writing. He is eager to support this and all subsequent materials with personal appearances, speaking engagements, classroom and seminar settings, radio, print, and any other media that will engage a wider audience. A website and blog has been launched in support of this book and ministry emphasis. It can be found at http://www.churchonenow.com.

For more information about
Jim Turner
&

SO-CALLED CHRISTIAN:
HEALING SPIRITUAL WOUNDS
LEFT BY THE CHURCH
please visit:

Website: www.churchonenow.com
Email: churchonenow@gmail.com
Twitter: @jimturner10
Facebook: www.facebook.com/jim.turner.94849410

....

For more information about
AMBASSADOR INTERNATIONAL
please visit:

www.ambassador-international.com
@AmbassadorIntl
www.facebook.com/AmbassadorIntl